SURVIVAL TIPS,
TRICKS AND
TRAPS

Wanda Priday
&
William Priday

SaltHeart Publishers, LLC

Copyright © 2020 SaltHeart Publishers, LLC
Published by SaltHeart Publishers, LLC

Illustrations by William Priday, unless otherwise noted

ISBN-13: 978-1944222024

Printed in the U.S.A.

Security is mostly a superstition. It does not exist in nature, nor do the children of men as a whole experience it. Avoiding danger is no safer in the long run than outright exposure. Life is a daring adventure or nothing at all.

Helen Keller

Knowledge weighs nothing.

Dedicated to the memory of my husband, William Priday.
Thank you for all the knowledge you shared with me and the time
we spent together to create this book.
Live on in all of nature forever.

Table of Contents

Chapter 1
What Would You Do?

You and your family must leave your home immediately, what essentials should you be in your bug out bag (BOB)? What are essential protocols to successfully bug out? During a without rule of law (WROL) scenario you have opted to bug in; how do you proof your home to increase the safety of your family and possessions? Get these answers and more in Chapter 2 EDCs, BOBs, Bug Out/In, & WROL

What are the initial signs of hypothermia? What can you do to avoid falling victim to it? How do you quickly create a shelter that will protect you from the elements? What everyday household items can be substituted during a 1st aid emergency? If you have an infection but no antibiotics or alcohol, what common foods and plants can you use as antibiotics and antiseptics? Someone in your family is desperate for pharmaceutical grade antibiotics but you can't access a doctor or pharmacy, learn how to access antibiotics legally without a prescription in Chapter 3, Earth Suit Maintenance.

You need to start a fire; do you know the different components that are needed and how to use them? Don't have a lighter or matches, learn how to start a fire in multiple ways: solar, electrical, chemical, friction and percussion. If your sticks and wood are damp, what common items can you us to accelerate starting and keeping a fire? Learn these answers and more in Chapter 4 Fire.

Lost in the woods, drank all the water in your pack but found a creek, how do you turn that into safe drinking water? Stranded in an arid environment or on a deserted island with nothing but ocean water, do you create a solar still, catchment device or distillation system for saltwater and how do you do that? Learn which purification method, whether it be chemical, filtration or distillation, is best for your situation and how to execute. Read how in Chapter 5 Water

All hell has broken loose, what tools do you need to take care of yourself? The answers might surprise you. If you don't have the essential tools, learn ways to improvise and create them from items in your environment. What is the best one tool option? What is the best survival knife? Want to know how to open a can without a can opener? How about how to make a sling shot with a condom and stick? How many ways can you use a hat to increase your survivability? Everyday tools that can help you survive are all around you, tips on how to spot and use them can be found in Chapter 6 Tools.

Society is changing and for many of us, it feels less predictable and potentially dangerous. If you are considering buying a firearm for personal protection or hunting, learn what type of firearm is best for your purposes. Learn what platforms are and how can they benefit you. All the basics needed are reviewed in Chapter 7 Firearms & Improvised Weapons so you can make an informed and comfortable firearm decision. In addition, discover tricks to create self-protection and hunting weapons that don't involve guns.

No phone, no compass, no problem. Learn how to navigate directions day or night without modern technology in Chapter 8 Navigation and Signaling. If you're traveling roads and interstates in the US, learn how the road numbering system conveys vital directional information. Need to be rescued? Multiple ways to signal for help are relayed in this chapter.

Chapter 9 Traps explains through illustrations and directions how to set up and catch small to large game, including fish and birds. Only have shoelaces or a strip of cloth from your shirt, learn how to set up multiple no-knife traps configurations. Need to catch and dispatch medium to large game for a protein source? If you have wire and a knife, you can create an effective snare trap on any game trail. Near a creek, river or on the coast, set up this passive, re-usable fish trap once and reap the benefits over and over. Want to catch a live bird? This dead-fall live trap will do the trick.

TERMS

<u>SHTF</u>: Shit Hit the Fan; implies an incident or event has happened to compromise our ability to obtain goods, services and emergency response necessary to maintain life as we had known it. This is considered an extreme social crisis scenario.

<u>WROL</u>: Without Rule of Law. A situation where emergency response services such as medical, fire and specifically law enforcement are not responding and probably won't for an extended period of time. This could be large scale rioting and civil unrest, an environmental or weather incident or outright societal system failure such as war - yes, war, it's been known to happen. Be armed and know how to protect yourself. If the police have stopped responding you are completely responsible for your own safety.

<u>EDC</u>: Every Day Carry. A bag or items you keep on your person,. It is a preplanned bag you keep with or near you at all times. The contents of your EDC should be regionally appropriate and easy for you to use. At the very least it should contain a cutting tool (knife), multi-tool (with saw, plyers, can opener, file, etc) fire starter (lighter or ferro rod) flashlight, water, seasonal appropriate clothing and shoes, and any medications and eyeglasses you may absolutely need.

<u>BOB</u>: Bail Out Bag or Bug Out Bag. A bag filled with enough food and gear to sustain you for about 72 hours.

<u>LNT</u>: Leave No Trace, meaning literally, leave no trace of your presence. LNT is a respect for your environment and the people and animals that will use it after you. It's common courtesy in parks and recreational areas. You are asked to pack out whatever you packed in, taking all your trash and even excrement with you when you leave. Reverse the concept of LNT and you will be leaving a trail of trash and other items behind you that may help you get located quicker.

RULES OF SURVIVAL

Survival is a game of percentages. Every skill that you learn is a percentage of improving your survivability. The more you know, the less you need to carry, the better chance of your survival. Most people live in denial about life's fragility and are unaware of how to provide for their most basic of needs outside of the current system. The most adaptable survive.

Everyone's survival situation will be different and the needs for each situation will vary. YOUR emergency happens where YOU are. A survival scenario can evolve quickly out of a simple roadside incident, inclement weather or power outages; common outdoor recreational activities can quickly lead the unprepared into emergency survival circumstances. Long term issues stemming from natural disasters, war, economic, political or infrastructure collapse coupled with emergency response service failure will raise a whole host of concerns. Our infrastructure is wholly dependent on electricity and gasoline; and we, as a society and individuals, are wholly dependent on that infrastructure. Electricity runs our lives, it has created amazing ease and allowed us to evolve, yet the importance of not being solely dependent could never be more immediate. Consider your everyday life and how you provide for your basic needs. We buy food from the store, we drink water from a pressurized tap, we flush the toilet for sanitation, we adjust the thermostat to keep ourselves warm and cool, all our needs are met by the push of a button. This is a new chapter in the story of human existence, we expect everything to keep being as it is. The reality is without our infrastructure, we will return to the wild, wild West in a heartbeat.

The infrastructure has created a bubble around each of us that protects us and provides for our needs. What if the bubble breaks? We will be left vulnerable and without proper supplies to care for ourselves. Common sense dictates we be prepared for short and long-term emergency and survival scenarios. Generations preceding us, as little as a hundred years ago, knew how to provide for their basic needs with their own hands. Back then, most people were entirely consumed on a daily basis with procuring for their basic needs.

There are some general rules to survival that everyone should keep in mind. When it comes to survival and efficiency, redundancy is key. 3 is 2, 2 is 1, 1 is none. Carry multiples of each essential survival item, such as knives, containers, fire starters, cordage, cover, etc. Items can break when subjected to harsh use, become lost or you may need to loan one out to a partner.

The basic guidelines for staying alive are:

RULE OF 3'S
Do not allow your body to go:
- 3 minutes without air
- 3 days without water
- 3 weeks without food

Death by exposure in freezing temperatures can happen in as little 3 minutes, your body temperature must stay extremely close to 98.6° F. Taking your body near the Rule of 3's limits will impair your ability to function, think and ultimately take care of yourself. If you exceed these time frames, you have diminished your strength and severely harmed your ability to get the water, shelter and food you will so desperately need in the coming hours, days and possibly weeks. It is a slippery slope when your physical and mental conditions are compromised in a survival scenario. Staying ahead of this curve is of paramount importance.

The Foxfire Series of 12 books and 2 anniversary editions is chocked full of historical no-nonsense Appalachian American know-how: simple yet efficient methods to living sustainably with the land. The Appalachian culture is closely linked to ancestral roots of the Medieval period in Europe from the 5th to 15th. These methods are time tested. And really, unless your bug out location is rigged with solar, wind or waterpower, be prepared for your lifestyle to be thrown back to the 19th century.

No one is an island. We are social creatures. Our primitive ancestors as individuals and societies. They didn't just wake up and find themselves born with all the knowledge one needs to survive. They were taught by their elders. Houses, food, tools, knowledge of seasonal harvesting and game migration routes were available and passed down. It was essential that each member learn their skills and participate as a community. What we would call "solo survival" today was called "banishment" then. Even if you are one of the few people who "solos" it, you didn't show up naked and build everything you have from scratch. Today we have become very specific in our knowledge of skills. True long term, self-reliance is a community built strong by the knowledge and skills of its members. If the grid really does go down and stay down for any length of time, prepare to be an asset to a tribe/clan/community. That is what it will take if you want to survive those changes. Understand that you will need people as much as they will need you. Skills that will be highly useful in a long-term scenario are fire making, sewing, blacksmithing, construction trades, engineering, 1st Aid and medicine, herbal medicine, wild foods, gardening, food preparation and preservation, hunting, sanitation practices and weaponry skills.

It may be difficult comprehending that "safety is an illusion". Truly understanding that phrase creates uncertainty and fear (referring to Helen Keller's poem). Humans by nature to do not like uncertainty. Fear is healthy and is an indicator to be aware and alert of ourselves and our environment. Unrestrained, fear can keep us in denial and leave us feeling powerless and possibly immobile. It is important to acknowledging that we live in a world full of contradictions to our safety. From that point we can begin to reduce the probabilities of danger through survival skills.

Having basic items, skills and knowledge are essential to effectively maintaining you, your loved ones and our collective society's wellbeing. This skill set gives you comfort, confidence and self-assuredness. Should we encounter a "grid down" event or an event without emergency responders, the more of us that know these skills the less traumatic that impact will be.

This is not an inclusive be all, end all, book on survival and all its related interests and fields. If one exists, we are not aware of it. The scope of such a book would cover an enormous volume of information. Just considering the differences in climate, geography, flora and fauna that exist globally and it's easy to see why no one has attempted to compile such an extensive work of this sort. Survival techniques and knowledge vary as much as climate and geography, from desserts to mountains, from tropics to arctic.

Compiled here are most of the survival tips and tricks we learned and used. These tips are meant to help increase your efficiency and survivability. Most of the techniques described in this book will work just about anywhere, but not absolutely everywhere. If you are looking for a survival 101 guide, attempt to obtain one for the type of region(s) you will be spending most of you time in. we strongly recommend hands-on field training from a reputable source, especially when it comes to wild edibles. We did not write this book specifically for any one type of person. Some of the topics and methods covered here are advanced, whereas others are fairly basic. These tips, tricks and traps are our field-tested favorites. It is our hope that those who reads this book whether a beginner survival student or a seasoned expert will discover new valuable lifesaving, energy-conserving, survival tactics.

This book touches on topics that volumes have been written on and serves as an introduction to new topics under the "survival" umbrella. The topic of survival can spin off into short and long-term emergency preparedness, primitive skills, hunting, security, sustainable living practices, homesteading, environmental consciousness, 1st aid and emergency medical treatments, trapping, shelter making, tool making and yes, even basket weaving. We encourage everyone to explore any survival topic that interests them, the more we all know, the more we will all be sustained.

Chapter 2
EDCs, BOBs, Bug Out/In, & WROL

When you need to use your survival skills, more than likely you will be under stress, possibly injured and in a precarious situation. Be prepared and have your EDC with you and your BOBs pre-packed and ready to go. Have your bug out and bug in plans made and review them with your family and friends.

EVERY-DAY CARRY (EDC)

These are the items you carry on your person, every day, at all times. An EDC can be condensed into the pockets of pocketed cargo pants, a small backpack, small bag or hip-pack.

The smallest EDC should at least contain 2 items: a fire starter (lighter, matches, ferrocium rod, fire piston, etc.) and a knife. The following checklist is recommended for a complete EDC.

CHECKLIST
- ☐ Knife
- ☐ Multi tool
- ☐ Lighters
- ☐ Micro Fishing Kit
- ☐ Mini Flashlight
- ☐ Whistle
- ☐ Mylar Survival Blanket
- ☐ Water Bottle(s)
- ☐ Eyeglasses
- ☐ Essential and Common Medications
- ☐ Identification & Copy of ICE (in case of emergency) contact list
- ☐ Snack bar(s)

BUG OUT BAG (BOB)

Each person in your group should have their own personal bug out bag. What you take with you will depend on your mode of travel. Have one in your car, office and house. Be ready from wherever you are. The short EDC checklist should be incorporated into the BOB checklist. The redundancies are intended. Your BOB becomes your EDC when you BO.

CHECKLIST

- ☐ Machete & Saw
- ☐ Small Spade/Shovel or Entrenching Tool
- ☐ Knife (duplicate)
- ☐ Multi tool (duplicate)
- ☐ Blade sharpener
- ☐ 550 cord
- ☐ Duct Tape
- ☐ Wire
- ☐ Surveyors Tape
- ☐ Cable Ties
- ☐ Bungee Cords
- ☐ Lighters (3)
- ☐ Candles
- ☐ Matches
- ☐ Flares
- ☐ Ferro rod/Mag bar
- ☐ Fishing kit (duplicate)
- ☐ 1st Aid kit, including suture kit, ace bandages, & moleskin
- ☐ Chapstick
- ☐ Whistle
- ☐ LED Mini flashlights/Headlamps/Lantern
- ☐ Batteries (AA, AAA, etc)
- ☐ Emergency USB charger
- ☐ Tarps/Shower curtains
- ☐ Additional Mylar Survival blankets

- ☐ 2-quart wide mouth metal bottle w/ metal top / Wide metal cup
- ☐ Food for 72 hrs – dried foods, peanut butter, drink mix, etc.
- ☐ Water for 72 hrs or as much as you can carry
- ☐ Water purification tablets/Water purifier or Life straw
- ☐ Extra clothes - seasonally appropriate
- ☐ Socks & Boots/Shoes you can walk comfortably in
- ☐ Jacket/Poncho
- ☐ Hat
- ☐ Heavy-duty Leather Gloves
- ☐ Extra Prescription Medications
- ☐ Antihistamines/Ibuprofen/Activated Charcoal
- ☐ Extra eyeglasses/Contact lenses
- ☐ Toilet paper/Napkins/Tissues/ Wet wipes
- ☐ Gallon Ziploc Baggies
- ☐ Maps/Compass
- ☐ Mini-Radio with solar or hand crank power backup
- ☐ Game/Book for comfort
- ☐ Childcare items as needed (diapers, sippy cup, blanket, etc)
- ☐ Quick start fluid/Fuel/Tablets
- ☐ Guns/Ammo
- ☐ 5-Gallon Bucket (packed with these BOB items)
- ☐ A Towel
- ☐ Hardcopy of Survival Tips, Tricks & Traps

EDC AND BOB TOOL TIPS & TRICKS!

Create a micro fishing kit using a plastic card (i.e. old gift card). Cut out notches on the short ends and wrap fishing line long ways, place fishing hooks on top and then duct tape around the card. Want to take it a step further? Drop your micro kit into an Altoids tin and now you have additional room for a sewing kit, some matches, a zip lock bag and a small lighter, use your imagination on what useful items you can include. When you are done packing the tin, duct tape or rubber band it closed. The tin, when empty is a small container that can be used to make char cloth. Instead of a tin, film canisters, snuff containers and

Chapstick tubes work well as micro kit containers for small items such as a fishing kit, water purification tablets, small candles, etc. A second small container can be loaded with petroleum jelly, cotton balls and matches to make an easy fire-starting kit. Read more in Chapter 4 Fire on this topic.

Tape a sharpening file to the handle of your spade or slide it into your machete sheath for easy access. Sharpening the sides of your spade will give you a decent chopping edge, much like an axe or machete and can be used as a weapon. It's not ideal, but it is a modification you can work with. The entrenching tool, depending on the model, can also serve as a mat axe or hoe, a pick and some of them have a sawing and chopping feature on them.

Surveyors' tape is versatile and tree friendly (better than blazing) as a marker for your trail or traps. It highly visible when signaling for rescue. Twisted and reinforced it becomes usable cordage or thrown into a fire, creates heavy smoke for signaling. Another signaling method is to attach multiple strands of the tape to a long stick and waving it for contrast and movement to get the attention of rescue personnel.

Cable ties are a small, lightweight item that can be used to bind together so many items. They can be melted down and reshaped into needed items, as well as, be a glue substitute. They also burn well for fire starting.

When creating your EDC or BOB, each item in your kit should have 2-3 different uses. Adjust and incorporate items you carry based on their multi-use. Example: A metal water bottle, doubles as a watertight storage device, a cooking pot, a water sanitation container and object for self-defense. You can also use it as a weight to throw rope or line up in a tree or across water, etc.

A food grade five-gallon bucket with an airtight rubber gasket lid is a must in your survival gear. Load it with your BOB supplies. It can serve as a water container, a flotation device, and a boiling pot (See Ch. 5

Water on how to), among other potentials. A backpack designed to carry a five-gallon bucket inside is highly recommended.

Bungee cords are ideal to use in many animal trapping systems. It can be used as the action instead of a spring snare or a counterweight style trigger system. It may also be used in conjunction with trapping systems as a force multiplier. Read more in Chapter XX, Traps.

Ziploc baggies provide waterproof containers for just about everything, however, do not carry gasoline in a Ziploc. Gasoline and a number of other petroleum-based products will melt through plastic.

A good pair of boots may be the most important piece of survival gear you own. Keep them waterproofed and break them in slowly before you where them for an extended period of time. If not, you will be sure to cause blisters that will be painful and limit mobility. Replace your bootlaces with 550 paracord. Melt the ends so they don't unravel. Double the laces with one continuous piece of cord allowing for twice the length in each lace. Small, useful items such as Ferro rods and fishing hooks can be slid into the end of paracord laces and then melted shut. Wrap a single-edge razor blade in a match book, wrap those in plastic and duct tape and insert under the liner of your boot. Add a fishhook or 2 and fishing line if you like. You can store multiple small survival items under the liner and in the soles of your shoes and boots.

BUG OUT TIPS!

When bugging out you will encounter less predictable circumstances, however in some cases it will be safer to relocate. Maybe your bugging out to get to a more remote location or to be with a community of other self-reliant people you trust.

Prepare and outfit your car for emergencies and survival in advance. If you become stranded while traveling, your car becomes your department store and your shelter.

Have an escape route, from everywhere, all the time. Make note of where you drive and the places and landmarks you pass before an emergency hits. Satellites may go down and GPS or navigation software is notoriously unreliable in remote areas. Do not rely on your navigation app.

Have multiple bug out plans that vary the mode of transportation (by vehicle, on foot, motorbike, bicycle, or boat) routes and possibly the location you are going to. If you live in an urban area, consider that people will be your biggest allies and adversaries, thus it makes sense for your group or family to get away from the hordes that will be vying for a small amount of resources. Staying in the city a few days might be wise, to gather your gear, friends, family and review your exit plans. Prearrange a location to meet family and friends at, in case cell phones are not working. From that meeting place, you can travel to a bug out/bug in location. Prepare that location and the route along the way with a cache of supplies to be used upon initial arrival. An ideal location will be one that can provide for you on a long-term basis because it has shelter with a heat source (fire, fireplace or stove), water, food sources and woods for building and heating fuel.

Have an emergency roadside kit in your car and know how to use it.

Have a good, inflated spare tire, a tire changing kit and learn how to change a tire.

Carry a can of fix-a-flat or 2 in your vehicle.

During a social crisis, stay alert while driving and understand that other drivers are stressed and distracted. Maintain a safe driving distance between yourself and other vehicles. Not only should you attempt to make this a daily practice, it could not be more important than in a critical situation. Leave enough room between your car and the one in front of you to maneuver into emergency lanes, onto the shoulder, sidewalk or median. When there is heavy traffic, or you are at a standstill, driving lanes could be permanently blocked.

A car can be stripped in a survival scenario to increase your survivability. Use the mirrors for signaling, the wires for cordage and the seats and mats for insulation. A car mat can become a sled to carry other items on, be made into a pair of flip flops, or as mentioned earlier in the book, used on a fire to create black smoke to signal rescue. Look at your car as a tool kit. Your car can be replaced, you cannot.

While having a clean car has its merits and comfort, a messy car could be your keys to survival. Just like a well-kept car, the messy car can be stripped of parts and used. However, the messy car is far more valuable in a survival situation. All that trash now becomes treasure, there may be stale food which is either bait or direct sustenance, fast food bags for fire starter, even the burger wrapper could be bait and containers like water and soda bottles will often have some liquid left in them and now has become suitable, but not necessarily desirable, option for caloric gain. A tin can is a container for cooking in, boiling in and sterilizing water. This list could go on and on and some of the items you may find or keep in your messy car have been addressed throughout the book.

Consider how the amount of trash alongside a road can give you information. More trash generally indicates higher road usage. Less debris indicates someone maintains the road or it is not often used. If all you see are beer cans, then you might set your guard up a notch and be wary of the types of people in that area.

A game you can play to increase your ability to adapt is to take note of roadside trash and debris and name/consider all the things they could be in a survival scenario. Look at what you see, don't label it trash, ask yourself, what can I use it for? A broken water cooler is a container, a float, a seat, insulation to keep you off the ground, a fire accelerant and signaling device. A metal hubcap is a plate, a grate, a signaling device, a shovel and plastic hubcaps will break to make a cutting edge. The proverbial plastic grocery bag (aka the urban tumble weed) becomes a carrying container, a rain hat, cordage, fire fuel or accelerant and when ripped into strips markers for your path.

BUG OUT TRAP!

Don't underestimate the difficulty of bugging out, especially if you live in an urban area. Your plan may be to load up your SUV with plenty of supplies, then head out with the family to your bug out location. However, roads that are congested during regular rush hour, will become clogged and impassable during an emergency evacuation forcing you to evacuate by foot and carrying all your supplies. Alternative roads may be impassable because of flooding or emergency activities. Be sure your bug out plan considered these potentials and pack efficiently. Consider the weight of your supplies and the ability of each member of your group to share the load and the distance. Should you be moving on foot, yard sailing (aka spreading all your stuff out) your supplies and repacking them on the roadside puts you at risk; exposing you to others that may want to commandeer your supplies.

Eighty percent of Americans currently are living in an urban-suburban area. The type of crisis, potential duration and your level of preparation will indicate whether you should bug in or bug out. Deciding where you can take best care of yourself and where you are safe should weigh heavily on your decision. If a crisis has knocked out power, emergency responders are will be inundated; a city will quickly become more dangerous. Vital resources: food, medicine and potable water will be depleted within a matter of hours. Grocery stores keep approximately 3 days of food in-stock, yet we have all witnessed the empty shelves before a storm. Don't rely on the store having food, if your planning to stay put at your apartment or suburban home, stock up on staples. You will need them.

BUG IN / WROL SECURITY

WROL scenarios mean the breakdown of society as we know it and if that happens personal security will be a high priority.

In a WROL scenario, cover your windows from the inside with dark material, such as black trash bags or dark blankets or sheets. A week or 2 into WROL and people will be looking to take advantage of those with supplies. Blacking out your windows keeps others from seeing movement or lights (flashlights, candles, etc.) which indicate your presence and may leave you vulnerable to attack.

Strew trash, furniture, debris and even feces on your lawn and porches to make your house appear as if it has already been looted and difficult to ingress.

Have stocks of ready to eat food to minimize cooking smells.
Be well armed. People regress when their lives are on the line and will be deadliest in WROL scenario. Read more in Chapter 7 Firearms & Security.

Stock up on toilet paper, alcohol, cigarettes and any medications, these will have value in WROL. Offering a cigarette or a drink could shift foe to friend.

Only keep pantry supplies that you can afford to lose to looters with you or in your home. Keep the remainder of your supplies in various caches that only you know their whereabouts.

One way to hide valuables in your home is to make those valuables look and smell as unattractive as possible. Place old clothes, trash and towels in piles on top of your stashes, then urinate and defecate on them – NO ONE will dig through a pile of crap just to see what might be there.

This theory works for people too. If you feel the need to, make yourself less of a target by smelling and looking bad. Urine, feces and alcohol on your clothes will keep others at bay.

Making rudimentary armor from household items will give you an advantage in hand to hand combat and serves as a good place to keep a blade. Bracers around your forearms made from several layers of cardboard or a phone book and duct tape. Slide butter knives in between the layers will fortify the bracers. Grieves are primitive shin guards and can be made the same as bracers.

Place crushed glass on the floor by your windows and doors of your domicile to create noise if someone walks through. It is not an alarm, but an alert, so you can ambush them instead of vice versa. Setting alarms, such as bells or glass jars above your doors will indicate to the trespasser that someone is present.

Place clothing against the bottom of your door. If it has been shifted or moved, it will indicate that someone has been there or is still there. Tape a strand of hair or strip of paper across the seam of windows and doors, so that if broken will show you someone has entered.

Whether you choose to alarm upon entry or silently alert after the fact depends on whether you want to deter, confront or evade.

Chapter 3
Earth Suit Maintenance

Earth suit maintenance is the ongoing process of maintaining your physical body; giving it what it needs to sustain life. Your body needs food, water, air and environmental conditions suitable to maintaining appropriate core temperature.

HYPOTHERMIA

Maintaining a body core temperature of 98.6°F is essential for your survival. If your body temperature drops below 96°F onset hypothermia is eminent. Hyperthermia occurs when body temperature is too high and reaches life threatening levels at 104°F. There is no other way to say it, maintaining a proper core temperature through hydration and shelter (clothing and/or cover) or fire is the most important element of your physical well-being.

Lack of shelter, water, and/or food will cause your temperature to exceed or drop below the desired mark of 98.6°F. Hypothermia, hyperthermia, and dehydration are your biggest killers in the outdoors, with hypothermia being the quickest to kill. When you are wet, you lose 25–30 times more body heat than when you are dry. If you cannot get out of the rain or warmed by a fire, depending on your constitution and physique, this could kill you.

Two ways to gauge whether you are going hypothermic are shivering and not being able to touch your thumb and pinky together easily. More often than not, hypothermia occurs at higher temperatures than we would normally think of. It doesn't have to be freezing for hypothermia to set in, rainy and 55°F without proper rain protection or clothing can lead to hypothermia. Geographical areas with extreme temperature fluctuations are where people have the highest risk of hypothermia. Someone out for an early summer day-hike in the Appalachian Mountains wearing shorts and T-shirt, where temperatures can easily soar to 80°F during the day and drop to the 40°F at night, will find they are severely underdressed come sunset. Desert and arid zone temperatures can also fluctuate drastically from the 100s°F during the day to 30s°F at night.

TIPS!

When going on day hikes, pack extra layers, should you be out when the sun sets, and temperatures drop.

If you are in cold weather conditions, be mindful not to break a sweat. When working at building a shelter, a fire or procuring food, you may work hard and work up a sweat. It may feel good to get the blood pumping and your body warmed up but sweat is dangerous. Once you stop moving and go to a sedentary position, the sweat then acts like a conduit and releases much needed heat from your body and can cause hypothermia to set in very quickly. Always work at a steady pace, strip off layers as needed and take breaks to avoid sweating. If you do find yourself sweaty, do all you can to wipe down and dry yourself off.

If your hands start to get cold and stiff slap them together very hard. The body senses this as trauma and sends blood to that area. This also works, strangely enough, in the heat for blisters on the hands. The increased blood circulation will allow the skin to reconnect and minimize the amount of blistering.

SHELTERS

The best shelters are what we call in the survival world, ma-nature specials. This is any type of space created by nature that is suitable for keeping one out of the elements – rain, wind, sun, etc. with little or no modifications needed. These can be caves, rock outcroppings, hedgerows, a natural cluster of trees or bushes or even a large fallen tree. Be aware that caves and rock outcroppings can be inhabited by bats and/or predatory animals. Bat and rat feces and urine create toxic chemicals. Breathing these toxins can cause histoplasmosis, a serious lung infection which can lead to death. Rodent droppings in general, have the potential to cause hanta virus and a number of other nasty, deadly viruses. Mountain lions will use caves for the same purpose as humans. If there is evidence of cat feces on the floor of a cave, be aware about clearing away the old, dry feces. Stirring up that dust can release toxoplasmosis which can be highly detrimental to one's health. Wrap fabric, dampened if possible, around your mouth and nose to reduce chances of breathing in these microscopic viruses.

When in a cave or under an outcropping, be aware of spalting rocks. If the rock walls and ceilings of caves are damp when heated by fire or frozen by low temps, shards and pieces can break off and fall. This is extremely dangerous and deadly. Look around the floor of the cave to see if there is evidence of previous spalting to determine if it is safe to build a fire. To increase the safety of a cave, allow a fire to burn for several hours inside the cave to warm up the rock walls and flush out any potential spalting rocks.

When setting up camp, always check for widow makers. This a dead limb, tree, boulder, ice shelf or snowdrift that could fall and impale or crush you. Storms, high winds and fire can dislodge them. Also be aware of camping in flash flood, tidal or mudslide/avalanche areas. Get above the flood line and do not stay in a slot canyon or ravine where rain turns instantly into roaring canyon rivers.

When building a shelter, always create a moisture barrier between you and the ground. The moisture in the ground will suck the heat right out of you. Carry a shower curtain or tarp in your BOB, build a raised bed or pile up leafy branches, grass or palm fronds at least 4" thick when compressed to be effective.

Button rocks are used to create a point of attachment for a tarp, curtain, blanket, etc. Take hold of the portion of the blanket or tarp where you want to create a point of attachment, place a small stone or bundle of foliage on the other side and wrap the blanket around the stone. Tie a piece of string/cordage, wrapped several times, around the stone and blanket. Then attach the other end to your pole or tree.

SLEEP

Sleep is vital to the body's normal functions. In a survival situation it may be impractical or impossible for you to sleep at the time you are most used to. Temperatures, weather, injuries and stress can have great effect on one's ability to rest. Taking power naps and sleeping whenever and wherever you can will help keep you charged up and your brain and body functioning well.

STAY COOL TIPS!

Your carotid arteries bring blood to the brain and are located in the neck near the skins surface. Avoid overheating by wetting a bandana or scarf (with urine if it's all you have) and wrapping it around your neck and head to cool these arteries that are taking blood to your head.

Heat and moisture are lost through your head, no matter what the temperature, so keep your head covered.   Although this seems counterintuitive, think of dessert dwellers and their use of scarves over their heads, keeping moisture in and reducing overall body temperature.

1st AID TIPS!

Any wound, whether minor or major, without 1st aid or emergency response services is potentially life threatening and severely impacts your ability to care for yourself and your loved ones. The best way to avoid injuries is to Simply Slow Down! Take your time moving around and when using tools.

Wear or keep appropriate and practical shoes in your BOB, car or at work for the season and climate you are in.

Mole skin is a must have for anyone that needs to walk a long distance. It takes up virtually no space in your BOB or EDC and can spare you a whole heap of agony. If you don't have mole skin and you get a blister you can create your own. Layer up several small squares of duct tape, cut out a circle in the middle the same size as your blister and apply over the blister, allowing blister to rise through the hole. This will reduce friction with your socks and shoes for a less painful trek. Leave it in place until your blister heals or you are able to go without shoes.

A blister can be drained by threading a needle and thread through the blister. Leave the thread in place. It will allow it to drain and keep the holes open for quicker healing.

Activated charcoal purchased at any drug store (or regular charcoal straight out of the fire if it is all you have) can be used as a digestive aid and can reduce diarrhea and other intestinal symptoms. Take about a half teaspoon and swallow. This can be repeated every few hours. Charcoal draws impurities and bacteria out of your system. It can also do some other amazing things. You can brush your teeth with it but be careful not to brush your gums too vigorously as it is abrasive. Rub it around your eyes to reduce glare and protect your eyes from bright sun or snow blindness.

If you are without a suture kit and stitches are required, use monofilament, dental floss (plain, not mint) or some other non-organic and preferably non-woven type of thread. Organic threads can often be interpreted by the body as foreign and may cause infection, irritation and prolong the healing process. Super glue is also a great alternative but be sure not to glue your fingers to the wound.

Tourniquets should never be used to stop bleeding unless death from blood loss is imminent. They will stop the bleeding but cause circulation loss to the whole limb resulting in limb death and gangrene (also ultimately a terminal condition) requiring amputation. Compression bandages should be used instead, whenever possible. Bind wounds tightly and maintain pressure until the bleeding has stopped. Either way it's a good reason to have an ace bandage and sanitary feminine pads in your first aid kit.

Plastic wrap or clear plastic have a multitude of first aid uses, such as a lung puncture to wound dressing, or burns. Burns treated with antibiotic ointment or salve and then wrapped with plastic will keep them protected from the elements, debris and lint. It removes the possibility of tearing skin when removing bandages, as burns scabs will stick to fibers.

Potassium permanganate, also known as KMnO4, Condy's Crystals and permanganate of potash, can be purchased at garden centers and hardware stores. Carefully add crystals to water one by one until the water turns purple to create an antiseptic solution, an anti-fungal treatment for the hands and feet and canker sores. Use caution and do not make your solution too potent, as it can cause burns to the skin.

Carry it in plastic containers as potassium permanganate is an aggressive oxidizer and will react with metal.

Should you need an antiseptic and do not have isopropyl alcohol, the following is a list of common and natural topical antiseptics:

Yarrow
Vinegar
Plantain
Pine sap
Juniper berries
Lemon
Grapefruit
Pineapple
Tea Tree Oil
Ground Black Walnut Husks
Thyme
Sage
Echinacea
Sphagnum moss
Any type of alcohol that is 80 proof or better

Out of this list (which in not all inclusive by any means) plantain, pinesap and yarrow are easily recognizable and found pretty much everywhere on the planet.

ENERGY EFFICIENCY TIP!

At the beginning of a survival situation harvest needed materials from as far away from your camp as possible. Even though you may anticipate a short stay, approach your situation as long term and be sustainable in your methods. As the days go by, your energy reduces from lack of nutrition, instead of going further away as you become weaker, you will travel shorter distances. It also gives you the added benefit of being able to recon the area which gives you more knowledge and opportunities to gather supplies in advance and therefore more options as you get weaker in a prolonged situation.

BUSH TUCKER TIPS!

Only over the last 200 or so years have processed and canned foods been available. Prior to that, food that was preserved was either dried, salted, smoked, candied, pickled or fermented. Most food was fresh, on the hoof or stored in root cellars or frozen in some way. The flavors you are used to today are not what was going around then. Try and keep this in mind and keep an attitude of being a culinary explorer. Different doesn't mean bad, just new. Bitter was far more common than sweet. Salt was so valuable that the Romans paid the legions in salt. It was called a "salarium". This where you get the word "salary" from. Peoples from the interior of continents used salty flavored plants to this effect. People ate bugs, rotten fermented shark and goats' heads that had been buried. All kinds of modernly offensive foods. While none of this seems super attractive; the nutritional value was often higher in some of these foods than common foods available today. You can go out in your yard and create a salad with higher nutritional value than anything you can buy at the store. So keep this in mind. Since corporations can't make a profit off of free, our societal conditioning leads us to have issues with anything that does not come out of a package. Food revulsion is a marketable tactic. What you generally consider "food" in all its prepared and prepackaged adornments is a new thing to the human race.

Knowing wild edibles is about harvesting schedules: knowing when to harvest what in your area. Research your climate and geography and find or make a chart for wild edibles. A useful harvesting chart for wild edibles would change weekly for multiple micro regions. Understanding the schedule of wild edibles is a substantial percentage in long term survival, should you not be able to stay in one place and protect a garden.

Pine needles make a very good vitamin C supplement and are available year-round. Use them to make a healthful, uplifting tea.

Earthworms have four to five times as much protein as a chicken egg. They are also high in iron, amino acids and calcium. They can be eaten raw, although not advisable. Cooked they taste a bit like bacon.

All thistle species, a high nutrient bush tucker that is easily found, can be eaten raw or cooked. When eaten raw the spines need to be scraped off. If braised on a fire, the spines will cook off and leave you with a tasty treat.

Wood lice (aka rolly pollies) taste like shrimp. termites and ants taste like lemon. All of these are protein sources that are easily harvested. They are found in composting logs, dead or dying trees and under rocks

Eating wild mushrooms should never be attempted for survival. Consider that even professional mycologists have been poisoned by misidentification. The caloric gain is not worth the risk. Avoid them and do not handle.

Avoid slugs, unless you are desperate for sustenance; if you do decide to dine on this less than savory tucker, be sure to gut and boil for at least 10 minutes. They are full of parasites and are known to feed on poisonous mushrooms and animal scat. Some folks consider Banana slugs tasty. If you are not familiar with different types of slugs or snails, then avoid them altogether. Another option is to harvest slugs and purge them, meaning isolate them alive, feed and water them non-toxic vegetation for a day or two to ensure they are safe.

Be diligent when hunting and gathering. Raw wild plants can be a hazard if not washed. Slug snot residue or trails on plants can give you parasites and eradicating those is a whole other topic. There are some parasites that actually make slugs snottier for that very reason. Parasites generally spend their lives in 4 or more stages and often change hosts for each stage. An example the Dicrocoelium dendriticum's, (aka tape worms) life cycle starts with a live reproducing adult found in sheep, cows, pigs and people. The eggs are passed by feces. Slugs feeding on contaminated dirt ingest them which causes respiratory issue, resulting in the slug emitting a snot-like ball containing the next stage in the parasites growth. Some ants really like this snot ball. The ants that are infected will then become little zombies climbing a blade of grass and hanging on to the tip and just staying there. Then they are eaten by a sheep or cow or human starting this cycle over again. The danger here being that if you ingest the parasite depending on which stage the of its life cycle, it can end up in a much worse places than your gut, like your muscles, your eyes or your brain. Not so bad if you are just trying to make it through 72 hours and can obtain medication soon, but plan on extensive problems if the parasite thrives in your system for long.

Always wash plants, clean and gut insects and animals. It's best to cook all bush tucker. Wash harvested plants, like stinging nettle, fiddle heads (aka spring time fern sprouts) and allow to wilt over a fire. Wilting is just exposing them to fire or heat until they shrivel up a bit. Fire will kill any parasites or bugs living on them, will singe the stinging hairs from the nettle or thistle, as mentioned above, and give the fiddle heads a more appealing flavor.

When identifying berries, there is an old saying: black and blue, 80% may be good for you, red and white, 50% dead by tonight. This is hardly a guide for someone unfamiliar with wild edibles and poisonous plants. Never eat anything you cannot identify. Just because the wildlife is eating it does not mean you can.

Wild edibles are regional and geographical. If you plan to eat wild edibles, research the ones in your area. Unless you know what you are eating, don't do it. Hungry is better than sick or dead. The wild carrot which is edible looks almost identical to a variety of hemlock plants that are poisonous and deadly. Wild carrot smells like a carrot, the poisonous hemlock does not.

There are several invasive species that are edible and grow in many places across the globe. The following are just a few to get familiar with.

Plantain weed (Plantago major) is entirely edible and is rich in magnesium, vitamin A, vitamin C, and vitamin K. As an invasive species, it grows everywhere. The leaves can be dried and stored or used fresh. It grows year-round. The seeds can be ground into flour and made into cakes or as a thickener in soup or stew. The leaves can be used to make a salve and into a poultice to fight and draw out infection when placed on a wound. To make a poultice simply add a few drops of water to the leaves and mash them up into a paste and apply. Most primitive or native peoples just chewed it up and put it in a wound then wrapped it. The leaves as well as the juice have been widely used as topical substances in poultices and lotions for treating sunburns, stings, insect bites, snakebites, poison ivy breakouts, rashes, burns, blisters, and cuts.

Furthermore, the leaves have also been heated and applied topically to swollen joints, sore muscles, sprains, and sore feet. It has also been used for many centuries in treating sore throats, coughs, bronchitis, tuberculosis, and mouth sores.

Studies have shown that plantain has anti-inflammatory effects and is also rich in tannin (which helps draw tissues together to stop bleeding) and allantoin (a compound that promotes healing of injured skin cells). Further studies have indicated that plantain may also reduce blood pressure, and that the seeds of the plant may reduce blood cholesterol levels. Plantain seeds were also widely used as a natural laxative, given their high fiber content. Teas made from the plant, were used to treat diarrhea, dysentery, intestinal worms, and bleeding mucous membranes. The roots were also recommended for relieving toothaches and headaches as well as healing poor gums.

There are many different species of plantain. Some, such as Rattlesnake Plantain, are more potent than others

Fig. 3-1 Plantain weed (public domain)

Wood sorrel (*Oxalis acetosella*) is tasty and has a strong lemony flavor. It is one of our favorite wild edibles; so much so that it is a regular at the kitchen table. It should be noted that it does contain oxalic acid, which in large amounts has been known to interfere with kidney function and cause pain in the joints. All of the research that's been done however, has led us to the understanding that you would have to eat a TON of it for it to be harmful. Infants and pregnant women should not consume it in great quantity. It also contains vitamin C, helping to ward off scurvy, colds, and infection. It contains quite a bit of moisture and was used by native peoples to alleviate thirst when traveling through areas without water. The leaves seeds/fruit and flowers can be eaten. Some species grow a tuber which can also be eaten. This plant grows almost globally with the exception of polar and extremely arid regions.

Fig. 3-2 Wood Sorrel (public domain)

Cat tail (Typha) is found along the edge of ponds and in wetland areas. It is a wonderful plant. It is always a water indicator. You may need to dig for it, but it is there. The root (a rhizome) and the stalk is where, throughout most seasons, the good stuff is. At the beginning of the root, there are small pointed protuberances called corms. Corms are the beginnings of next year's shoots and can be eaten raw or cooked. The root is like a rope connecting the cat tails together. It will need to be dug up and baked. This can be accomplished by just throwing them on top of some coals and turned occasionally or buried in the fire under a few rocks. Peel open the outer casing and eat the starchy portion inside. There will be stringy material in there too. Just suck the pulpy stuff off and don't eat the strings. Digging them up is hard, cold work in the winter but after you get the first few out it becomes much easier. When the large seed pod is green it is edible. Grind it up into a paste with a little water and make cakes out of it. Bake on a flat hot rock or build a primitive stone oven. It can also be ground and used like flour to thicken soups and such. When they are brown and dry, it can be used whole as a punk for transporting a burning ember. Or break them up to use for insulation or fire tinder which takes a spark nicely.

Fig. 3-3 Cat Tail (public domain)

Cat Tail stalks can be used as a hand drill for fire by friction, harvest it green then allow to dry thoroughly.

The leaves can be made into cordage, its suggested to watch a few videos or researching further. It's a bit technical. Broad leaf Cat Tail requires splitting the leaves. Narrow leaf Cat Tail does not. You will need to break up the fibers a bit by folding it long ways. Dry it out then re-wet it before using it.

The world-renowned weed, dandelion (Ta-raxacum), is on our list of wild edibles. The entire plant, including the roots, stems, leaves and flowers are edible but bitter. Its leaves are less bitter before it blooms. They can be eaten raw or cooked like greens or harvested and dried. Dandelions are high in vitamins A, B, C & D.

They also contain iron, potassium and zinc. Dandelion tea makes a comforting and cleansing tonic. It has been used by primitive peoples as an appetite stimulant and as a treatment for liver, stomach, gall bladder, kidney and stomach problems. It is also a diuretic. Some studies show that it helps regulate blood sugar levels being helpful to diabetics possibly. Good thing to know. The roots have long been cleaned then dried and ground for use as a coffee substitute or just to strengthen coffee flavor. All of this being said if you are allergic to latex, some people may have an allergic reaction from touching dandelion. Others may get mouth sores. If you are allergic to ragweed, chrysanthemums, marigold, chamomile, yarrow, daisies, or iodine, you should avoid dandelion.

Fig. 3-4 Dandelion (public domain)

Clover is another globally available plant that is edible. It's an exceptional plant in that it has protein in it. It also contains vitamins B and C and beta carotene. You can eat the flowers and leaves raw. The young leaves are better. It can also be cooked liked spinach which is what is recommended. The roots should be roasted.

Some warnings concerning clover: 1. Some people are allergic to it. 2. NEVER eat fermented clover. It will probably kill you. Eat it fresh or dried. Never in between. This means do not snack on it while its drying. 3. Clover in warm climates can contain cyanide. It's considered a famine food. The flowers are the only tasty part eaten in any quantity. It's not bad if you are just eating a few leaves but it doesn't taste good if you have a mouth full of it.

In general, be sure to do your research and identify plants without doubt before you consume.

ANTIBIOTICS

An inexpensive, non-prescription and legal way to obtain antibiotics is to purchase veterinary antibiotics. Whether you want to stock up for a SHTF scenario or become more self-reliant in your daily life, you can purchase veterinary antibiotics at a pet store or online without a prescription. Here is a list of human antibiotics, their veterinary counterpart and common infections. Dosage amounts are based on age, weight, other medications in use and type of infection an individual may have. Most antibiotics are used in courses of 7 – 10 days. Dosage amounts can be found in the Physician's Desk References (PDR). Older hard copies can be found in thrift shops and used online bookstores. It's a good reference book to have on hand. There is also an online searchable version.

Veterinary to Human Antibiotic Conversion Chart

Pharmaceutical Name/Dosage	Veterinary Name	Used to Treat
Amoxicillin 250mg	FISH-MOX	Bronchitis, Ear infection, Gonorrhea, Lyme disease, Pneumonia, Skin infections, Throat infections, Tonsillitis, UTI
Amoxicillin 500mg	FISH-MOX FORTE	
Ciprofloxacin (Cipro) 250mg	FISH-FLOX	Skin infections, Sinusitis, UTIs, Prostatitis, Pneumonia, Bone and joint infections, Diarrhea caused by bacteria, Gonorrhea, Typhoid fever
Ciprofloxacin (Cipro) 500mg	FISH-FLOX FORTE	

Pharmaceutical Name/Dosage (cont.)	Veterinary Name (cont.)	Used to Treat (cont.)
Cephalexin (Keflex) 250mg	FISH-FLEX	Respiratory tract, Middle ear, Skin and Bone infections, and UTIs
Cephalexin (Keflex) 500mg	FISH-FLEX FORTE·	Respiratory tract, Middle ear, Skin and Bone infections, and UTIs
Metronidazole (Flagyl) 250mg	FISH-ZOLE	Parasitic infections including Giardia, Amebic dysentery, Liver abscess, Bacterial vaginosis, Trichomonas vaginal infections, Pelvic inflammatory disease, Stomach or intestinal ulcers
Doxycycline 100mg	BIRD-BIOTIC	Dental infections, Skin infections, Respiratory, UTIs, Acne, Lyme disease, Malaria, and Chlamydia
Ampicillin 250mg	FISH-CILLIN	Ear infections, Bladder infections, Pneumonia, Gonorrhea, E. coli, Salmonella infection, Meningitis, Infections of the stomach or intestines
Ampicillin 500mg	FISH-CILLIN FORTE	
Sulfamethoxazole 400mg/ Trimethoprim 80mg	BIRD-SULFA	Middle ear infections, Respiratory infections, Intestinal infections, UTIs, Traveler's diarrhea, Shigellosis, Pneumocystis pneumonia (fungal infection of the lungs)

SANITATION

Sanitation is critical in both emergency survival and long-term WROL situations. Keeping yourself clean and any wounds cleaned and bandaged will improve your survival. Cholera and diphtheria will be rampant in urban SHTF scenarios.

Before an emergency hits, set up rain catches and store water. Toilets will flush even when the electricity is out, simply pour 1-2 gallons of water in the back of the toilet and then flush or pour directly and quickly into the bowl. Remember, this does not have to be potable water; it can be rainwater or recycled from washing the dishes or yourself. To displace the amount of fluid required for a flush place a large dense object, such as a couple bricks or a jug filled with rocks and water, so it won't float, in the back of the toilet. Limit the number of flushes per day. If its yellow let it mellow, if its brown flush it down. Your survival sanitation protocol may require that, believe it or not, you coordinate with other household members on the "brown" for further flush reduction.

When outdoors, always relieve yourself at least 200 feet away from any water source (spring, stream, river or lake) to avoid contamination. If you are going #2, dig a hole about 6 – 8 inches deep, do the deed, then replace dirt and cover with debris such as leaves. For long term stays outdoors, dig a privy 2 -3 ft. deep, add leaves and dirt to compost the layers.

Run out of toilet paper or tissues? Moss is a soft natural toilet paper and hand sanitizer. It's antibiotic and cleansing properties keep your hands and your bum fresh and sanitized. Sphagnum moss with it's high acidity that does not allow for microbial growth is used for wound care. Doubly, tis absorbency allows it to be a water-source and feminine hygiene product. Mullein leaves have multiple uses because they contains a demulcent, emollient and astringent properties which when made into a tea or dried and smoked can relieve symptoms of bronchitis, asthma, pneumonia, pleurisy and whooping cough. Similar to moss, Lambs ear is antibacterial, antiseptic, anti-inflammatory and absorbent. Both Mullein and Lambs ear plants are soft, dry and pleasant on the skin.

Fig. 3-5 Mullein plant (public domain)

Fig. 3-6 Lambs Ear (public domain)

Fig. 3-7 Sphagnum Moss (public domain)

Chapter 4
Fire

Fire has been humans' primary tool for tens of thousands of years. Only in about the last 130 years has the Western world substituted electricity for fire and all the purposes it serves. It has been and always will be a multi-tool. Fire provides light in the dark, heat to keep you warm, a way to sterilize water, a way to cook food, a tool to process and create other tools, a communication signal, a hunting implement, a weapon, a first aid tool for cauterization and sterilization and of utmost importance, psychological comfort. Fire is still used by many cultures to clear land. It is done to remove brush for agricultural purposes and for hunting by clearing overgrowth and brush which promotes fresh, new growth that grazing animals are drawn to. Clear of underbrush, the area is now easier to locate and accurately shoot game. It allows hunters to retrieve their arrows, bolts, throwing sticks, etc. A burn off will herd, drive or kill game animals and creates fertile hunting grounds. A fire's smoke is an insect repellent, a cleanser, and a way to preserve meat. Natives would smoke or smudge themselves and their clothing to remove odor, insects, bacteria and fungi. Fire is critical to survival. Knowing how to start and maintain a fire in all types of conditions is a huge percentile of survival.

We learned to capture and carry naturally occurring fire first, eventually stone knapping led us to discover sparks when certain rocks are struck against each other, this is the most likely way we 1st learned to make fire. Much debate remains on when these stages of relationship between humans and fire occurred and for how long.

After this initial accidental flint and steel discovery (iron pyrite/quartz) for creating fire, countless configurations of fire by friction followed, configurations dependent on the resources available in any given location. Just to name a few: hand drill, bow drill, fire plow, fire churn and pump drill. Some preferred dried woods are aspen, bamboo, cedar, cottonwood, cypress, juniper, walnut, willow and the yucca plant.

Learn to build and work with fire (of course, in a safe and responsible way). Learn what fire is about, how it works, how it burns, become familiar with this most valuable, lifesaving tool.

Fire consumes air, be mindful of combustion in closed spaces or indoors. Oxygen deprivation kills you without you even knowing it by inducing a sleep you don't wake up from.

COMPONENTS OF A FIRE

These three elements are needed to create fire.

Fig. 4-1 Fire Components (public domain)

The following is a list of terms and definitions for the different types of fuel.

Tinder: The lightest material used to start a fire with. Tinder should be able to take a spark and either smolder or light a flame. It can be shredded paper, cotton or light fluffy plant material. When you are looking for tinder outdoors, look for plants with fluffy or cotton like heads, such as dandelion, cat tail, milkweed, and thistle; sometimes fluff can be found inside large seed pods. Bird and rodent nests generally make great tinder, but beware, animal hair does not make good tinder and smells awful when burned!

Kindling: Small dead or dry twigs, split sticks or shavings, about the size of pencil lead. Save shavings from carving projects, like making a spear or a trap set.

Sticks: Dry dead pencil to finger size twigs and branches.

Logs/Firewood: Large wrist size sticks, small trees and chunks of wood that are the main fuel source.

Accelerant & Extenders: Items that assists in starting and maintaining a fire, some examples are gasoline, alcohol, perfume, paint thinner, petroleum jelly, shoe polish, rubber, Chapstick, wax, pine sap, fatwood, etc.

TRICKS TO STARTING A FIRE!

Fire is created 5 different ways: optical/solar with a lens, electrical, chemical, percussion (i.e. quartz against carbon steel) and friction (i.e. bow drill).

OPTICAL / SOLAR

Projection TV sets from the 80's, contain a Fresnel lens as the screen. They also make them in many other sizes for magnified reading, etc. Book stores and craft stores carry various sizes that will be weightless in your B.O.B. Use it to start a fire and even cook with in bright sun.

Magnifying glasses, camera lenses, eyeglasses and binocular lenses can all be used to potentially start a fire with bright sun. Adjust them above a tinder bundle so that the sunlight is concentrated into a small point. Don't be afraid to break your binoculars or camera to get the lens out, it can be replaced however you cannot.

Lightbulbs can also be used to create a lens that provides magnification and a concentrated small point of light to start a fire. Use a standard size lightbulb or larger, larger is better. Using a clear lightbulb would be optimal, but many have an opaque coating on the inside. To remove this coating, first remove the filament and internal electrical elements,

To remove the filament, remove the aluminum disk from the bottom of the lightbulb, then carefully chip away the black glass that was surrounding the aluminum disk enough to create an opening to remove the filament and elements that are inside the bulb. Put a small amount of sand into the bulb and swirl it until it has removed the opaque coating and becomes clear. Fill the lightbulb with clear liquid to create a lens that will give you a focal point of sunlight.

An aluminum can may be used with the sun to start a fire. This trick takes chocolate, toothpaste or wax as a means to polish the can. Apply the polishing agent to the bottom of the can and polish with a rag until it has a mirror finish. Place the tinder bundle between the can and the sun. Focus the pinpoint reflection from the can onto the tinder bundle and hold until it begins to smolder.

A clear ice wedge or lens made from ice can also create a focal point of light and heat enough to start a fire, but be careful, don't let it drip on your tinder. Use ice that is solid with as few air bubbles in it as possible. Another method for starting a fire with ice is by creating an ice ball. Use a pipe end, can or metal bottle to carve the ice out in a circular motion to create a cylinder, and then continue to refine the cylinder until you have a sphere or ball. Polish the surface of the sphere using your hands which will slightly melt the surface, giving you a smooth finish. Try to make it as large as possible so that it will refract more light and create more heat. This is not an easy method to pull off, but it is possible. Gloves are almost a must for shaping and holding the lens. Once it is built put a handle or frame on it to hold it, something as simple as a vine or a green stick wrap.

Fire can also be achieved using clear plastic, such as cellophane or garbage bags. You will need to construct a square shaped frame and attach the plastic, like you are putting glass in a large picture frame except you use plastic and secure it all the way around the edge. Mount the frame off the ground, using four forked sticks as a stand. Pour water into the frame, the weight of the water will create a belly and function as a lens. The height will need to be adjusted so that the focal point is off of the ground. You are not going to be able to move the frame like you would a magnifying lens so noon day sun directly overhead will give you the best focal point. For the same reason you will need to move your tinder bundle to the focal point and add mass underneath the tinder bundle (rock, wood, etc.) to set it in place if you aren't going to hold it. Be careful to watch the process carefully. You will want to remove the tinder as soon as it catches, otherwise, you can melt the plastic and water will splash down and put out your embers. This method takes some practice which can be a fun one to do in the back yard with the kids

A condom or clear bag filled and tied tight with clear liquid and a bright sun can be turned into a lens to start a fire with. Make it as spherical as you can. Hold it between the sun and your tinder bundle, adjust till the sunlight is pinpointed on the bundle, hold there until an ember begins to burn.

ELECTRICAL

A battery can create enough heat to start a fire. Touch the positive and negative ends of almost any battery (including a cell phone battery) with wire, steel wool, a strip of aluminum foil, a foil backed gum wrapper, a wire bread tie, or the foil from a cigarette pack to create heat enough to light a very fine tinder. If using a foil with paper, cut it into an hourglass shape so the resistance is greatest in the narrow center. This is not an easy method and can burn your fingers; you may want to practice this in advance and always wear gloves to protect your fingers from burns. Using steel wool is the easiest to light tinder, gum wrappers and lightweight materials burn quick and hot. Have the metal touch the tinder as you connect the ends to the battery. A cigarette or cigar can be substituted for tinder to create a slow burning ember. With the exception of car batteries, the batteries used need to be relatively new to provide enough electrical charge.

The surface of cylinder batteries such as D, C or the multiple variants of A. is part of the positive terminal. By just scratching through the plastic cover near the negative end and touching the exposed metal and the negative end with a very short piece of wire will heat up enough to ignite tinder. Gloves are recommended for this trick so you don't burn your fingers.

Jumper cables attached to the battery on one end and tapped together at the other will create sparks that create a fire. A highly flammable accelerant like gasoline or very fine tender such as cotton balls or char cloth will be needed. This is also dangerous and can cause your car battery to explode. Remove it from the vehicle and then move as far away from the battery as the cables will allow before attempting. Another helpful tip when attempting this method is to use a smaller piece of wire (like speaker wire, a nail or coat hanger) in one of the cables to make the connection. Because of its smaller diameter it causes more resistance and heats up quicker than the cable wire, will become red hot and even possibly burn off into your tinder. Use caution and remember fumes can be explosive. Use caution and remember that gasoline fumes are explosive.

CHEMICAL

A chemical reaction fire can be made by mixing potassium permanganate with glycerol. These 2 ingredients are often found in traditional 1st aid kits (more on that in Earth Suit Maintenance chapter) Potassium permanganate is sometimes an ingredient in flower stay-fresh packets and antifreeze contains high amounts of glycerol. Place equal amounts together on a flat surface, stir together and then stand back. Wait nearby with tinder in hand, once the chemical fire has started; add tinder, twigs and small sticks to build your fire up.

PERCUSSION

A fire can be started using virtually any firearm that uses gunpowder. The first thing you want to do is create a very, large pile of dry leaves, grass and tinder, approximately as much as would fill a large black trash bag. Place the pile in front of a back stop, such as a tree, rock or bank then create a barrier to keep debris from flying everywhere when you shoot it. This could be sticks around the pile of leaves or even leaves placed in a trash bag. Next, prepare your ammunition. While holding your shell casing, bullet pointed upward, pry or pull out the bullet from the casing. Be careful not to spill the powder, but you may need to pour a little out depending on the round. Load the shell with combustible materials or fabric, such as tinder or cotton; this will keep the powder in while you are pointing the gun downward to shoot it. Make SURE the safety is on, and then add some marginally sized pieces of cotton into the barrel all the way down against the shell. Use a narrow stick or reed to poke it down. Don't cram it in, but make sure it is secure and firm, you don't want the wad to fly out before it catches. Get about 10 feet away from the leaf pile and shoot towards the bottom of it. Sometimes the flaming cotton never even makes it to your leaf pile. So, be ready to jump on that radiant flame. With shotguns, it's the same process; just remove all the shot.

FIRE BY FRICTION

Many people with an interest in outdoor survival want to learn the quintessential - fire by friction. It will take most of a day to locate the right wood, create the pieces and create an ember.

There are plenty of internet resources where you can watch the various methods, such as the bow drill, hand drill, pump drill, bamboo slide set, fire churn, bamboo fire saw and more. But just because you have seen it done, doesn't mean you can do it. Fire by friction takes patience, practice and tenacity.

If you haven't practiced fire by friction, it is not likely to happy for you the 1st time in the field.

FIRE BY FRICTION TRAP!

Don't have your fire attempt fail because you are not experienced at creating flame from an ember. Making a fire set is difficult, if by chance you get an ember by friction, you will have put a lot of effort into creating that ember. Before you try making a fire set, practice finding wild tinder and learn how to start a fire with an ember in a tinder bundle/bird's nest first! Use a cigarette, incense, or cigar ember to practice with.

BOW DRILL TIPS!

First bow drill tip: Carry a lighter

The bow drill can do more for you than just start a fire. Its' multiple functions make it worth investing the time and energy to create one. It can start fires and drill holes. The bow as an "engine" can be employed to open or shut gates, work as a bellows and serve as an engine for the axel of a water wheel.

The bow drill fire set components are bow, spindle, bearing block, hearth board, and catch plate. By modifying the bearing block and adding a rail you can increase your efficiency. Instead of a hand-held bearing block use an entire stick and brace it against a tree or other stable object, see Fig. 4-2. Adding a rail reduces exerting energy on the bows position and allows your energy to go to the back and forth motion rather than having to control the up and down motion at the same time. The bow should rest horizontally to your hearth board.

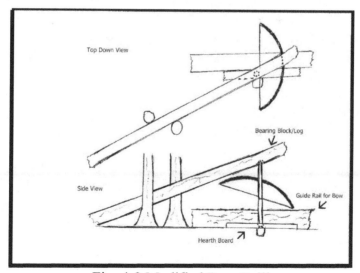

Fig. 4-2 Modified Bow Drill

In Fig. 4-2 the bow is not represented in the position on the rail. Imagine dropping the bow down until it contacts the rail and keep your hand horizontal to the rail.

Imagine rapidly sliding a broom stick at a 45° angle back and forth across the edge of a table, remove the table and the top of the stick will wobble. A lot of energy will be spent trying to keep the end of the stick level rather than the movement.

How to hold your bow: while grasping the end of the bow, place your index and middle finger around the string. Use these fingers to change the tension in the bow string as it heats up, loosens or tighten as you exert motion on the bow. Fire by friction is not easy under the best of circumstances, so be persistent and patient.

FIRE TIPS!

Don't have the longest, most uncomfortable night of your life should you find yourself in a survival situation after dusk. Always be prepared and have a flashlight, headlamp or lantern with you so that you can build a much-needed fire in the dark. It is very difficult, especially in a stressful situation, to start a fire in the dark without a flashlight. Even collecting additional firewood throughout the night, is prohibitively difficult using a homemade torch. A fire at night is critical to your productivity, physical well-being and your psychology. It enables you to see at night around your camp and create needful items such as traps, signals or cordage which allows time to pass more quickly and ease your mind. It gives you a sense of security when nature goes bump in the night. And, of course, a fire keeps you thermo-regulated.

Prep work is everything when building a fire. Collect at least two or three times as much tinder, kindling, and sticks than you think you need. It will burn faster than you anticipate. You don't want to lose your fire because you had to leave it to collect more wood.

Plan to protect your fire from the rain. The weather may be fine now, but it is subject to change quickly. Large stumps, slabs of wood and large pieces of bark placed directly on top of your fire create a natural awning. Identify and gather these pieces of wood then set them aside should the rain or snow start. Another method to protect your fire, is place leaves over a cooking rack. One can be made by placing 3 or 4 forked sticks in the ground around your fire, fork up and then lay sticks across them. Make sure your rack is built at a reasonable height and size, so it won't catch fire.

You may find yourself creating a lot of shavings while carving or processing wood. It may be tempting to scatter them or just throw them in the fire - don't. Keep them in a single area and use for kindling. Designating a workstation where you do your carving and chopping will help keep a healthy supply, so you can put your energy to better use later.

The best and most important advice is to carry lighters, preferably with an adjustable flame! Tried and true choice is Bic lighters which are robust and durable. Have one or two in your pocket, your car, your office and your home. Fire by friction or alternative fire-starting methods are prohibitively difficult regardless of what you have seen on TV. Spending $3 on a pack of lighters may very well save your life. There is no reason not to carry such a small, lifesaving item with you at all times. Another note on disposable lighters, if you do not use one daily, it is best to carry them upside down in a lighter case. Why? Because while in your pocket or purse, it is possible for the lighter trigger to be depressed and the gas leak out of the lighter and it will keep your lighter dry if you take an inadvertent dunking. It is by no means waterproof, but it helps. If your lighter does get wet remove the guard and any childproof safety features. Shake it. Replace the guard and run it quickly down your pants in the striking direction, this friction will dry out the inside components.

Short of a lighter, a magnesium bar with a ferrocerium striker (a.k.a. ferro rod) is probably your best option for getting a fire started in any weather. Assuming you didn't wait until dark and provided high winds aren't blowing your magnesium shavings around, it will handle just about anything else. Outright drenching rain and snow are no match for this combo. Pick one up. They are inexpensive and compact. The only downside to ferro rods is that they will corrode and rust in and near saltwater. Even salty air will quickly affect them. The flint from lighters is also made from ferrocerium. Keep this in mind and keep yours in a heavy-duty watertight container or chose another option if you are near saltwater.

Zippo style lighters are a great option for quick and sustained light and fire. Most of the nicer models are reasonably water resistant. They do however need a bit of upkeep, even if not used, as the fuel will evaporate over time. The trick to using a Zippo is to carry extra fuel for them. Use a small squirt bottle with a screw off top, like a Visine bottle. Fill it with lighter fluid just like you would use a turkey baster. Carry spare flints under the first layer of cotton in the insert where the lighter is refueled.

FIRE EXTENDERS

Using a fire extender in the process of lighting a fire can be helpful when it is damp or windy. Here are a few tricks:

Almost any liquor over 100 proof (50%) burns well. Higher proofs may even ignite from sparks alone.

Fritos, Cheetos, Doritos and potato chips are saturated with flammable oil. Light one on fire and see how helpful they can be!

Rubber bands, alcohol-content hand sanitizers, duct tape, tires, many types of footwear, Styrofoam, super glue and its fumes are all flammable and can assist in starting a fire.

Petroleum jelly, Chap Stick, lipstick, wax, antibiotic ointment, shoe polish and a variety of other creams, salves and deodorants are flammable. If combined with a tampon, cotton ball or piece of cotton shirt/bandana, a respectable fire extender is created. Keep cotton balls and petroleum jelly in a film canister for an easy start.
Crayons are a great fire extender and can also be used as emergency candles. Melt the flat end and adhere the crayon to a flat surface, and

then light the top. The paper coating acts like a wick.

Save old birthday candles for easy fire start, wind proof candles are optimal. Both are effective and small enough to fit into an Altoids tin.

Birch bark will light when it is wet and/or green.

A variety of tree saps are also flammable, such as pine, fir, spruce and cedar.

CAUTION!

Gasoline fumes are explosive, not the gas itself. Stay upwind and use caution when lighting a fire using any type of accelerant.

If Mother Nature is the one controlling the fire, then get upwind of the fire or into water, submerge yourself and remain calm. Use a piece of wet clothing as a face mask. Stay out of the smoke. Get low. Smoke kills more people than fire. If you have no body of water or any other choices, then do a burn of your own. Face away from the wind. Light a fire. If you need to do this there should be plenty of dry material around you. Once you have burned an area, move into the burned-out area. It gives the wildfire nothing to consume near you. If it's a "wet your pants moment", use your urine to wet a piece of clothing and breathe through it. You may live to tell your grandchildren and gross them out.

TRICKS FOR MAKING YOUR FIRE EFFICIENT!

When building a fire, lay logs or stones on the ground under the fire lay as a moisture barrier. This improves the fire-starting process and creates more coals.

If making a fire in deep snow, dig down to the ground if you can, or use green/live logs 4 – 6" in diameter and roughly 3 feet in length, lay them parallel until you have a 3' by 3' fire lay. This will require an axe or a saw. You can use dead wood, but because the dead wood will burn easier, green wood is preferable. If you do not have a base or do not dig down to the ground, your fire will sink through the snow and extinguish.

In the beginning stages of starting a fire it is necessary to break up tinder, kindling, medium size sticks and a few logs into manageable pieces, but after the fire is established, no more firewood needs to be processed. You can lay multiple 10 ft. logs across the fire and let the fire burn them in two for you, then lay those sections on the fire, or feed the logs in from one end. Do not spend the calories busting up logs if you don't need to! A nice neat pile of firewood is not what it takes to have a fire, just wood, in any manageable length.

CHARCLOTH

Dry charred materials take a spark or ember easily. Create char cloth using a metal container that seals. A metal thermos, a tin can, a metal bottle, an Altoids tin, or a salve container are all good options. Place a piece of charrable material in the container. Charrable materials are previously charred wood, cotton (from a t-shirt, bandana, socks or underwear), denim, and bracket fungus. Synthetic materials or animal fibers are not well suited to make char. Place a pin-size hole in the container if needed or leave the lid ever so slightly loose; this will allow gases to escape. Place the tin in a fire. Watch the gases escaping until they stop smoking, then you know your char is ready. Do not use plastic tops. If you do not have a top and are using something such as an aluminum or tin can, simply dig a small hole, put the cloth inside the can and then flip it upside down into the hole. Fill dirt in around the can leaving a little space for gas to escape. Move the coals from the fire and place on top of and around the can. Stop the combustion process by removing the container from the heat and allow it to cool. The cloth inside will now easily take a spark. Make sure you try your char cloth BEFORE putting out your fire and moving on.

SO, YOUR LIGHTER IS DEAD OR IS IT?

A dead lighter, even one that seems to have no fuel, is by no means useless. To access residual fuel, remove the metal guard and any child proofing from the front of the lighter. Often there is still a little fuel in the lighter. By removing the guard and striking, you may get 2 or 3 more lights out of it.

If it is an adjustable lighter, run the adjustment to the high position then pop the adjustment collar off, while disengaged move the collar back to the low setting and re-engage it to the gear and run the gear and collar back to the high position. It is like how you use a full-face wrench in a position where you cannot go a full 360 degrees, you have to lift the wrench (collar) up and off and reset it. This does not work on lighters with a metal wheel adjustment; in this case, spin the wheel towards the high position as far as it can go.

A completely dead lighter, with its wheel and flint intact will still create sparks and light char cloth or cotton fibers. Create flint shavings that light by rolling the striker wheel slowly in the standard lighting direction so it doesn't actually combust or spark. This will grind off ferrocium/flint with the striker wheel and allowing the flint pieces to fall onto a paper. Condensed into a small pile of concentrated material, add to tinder for easy combustion when you strike the lighter for a spark.

Chapter 5
Water

Over 70% of the Earth's surface is covered by water and about 97% of it is saltwater. Of the remaining 3% fresh water, 65 – 70% of that is frozen in the polar ice caps. That means that only about 1% of the Earth's fresh water is accessible to humans. Large quantities of that are chemically polluted from the effects of industry and what has followed. Water is a precious, life giving commodity.

Water is the most important resource to humans, whether you are in a survival situation or not. Entire civilizations have risen and fallen due to the availability of water. Generally, major cities were originally founded with a small settlement near a reliable water source.

Before modern pumping stations, humans were closely linked to water sources. Water has been and always will be essential to human life. This is why in survival philosophy when you find a stream, you follow it, and eventually you will find civilization.

Stay hydrated. Keep water with you as a daily habit. In optimal conditions, adequate intake of water for males is 3 liters per day and for women it is 2.2 liters per day. Increase this amount if you are exerting intense physical energy or there are drastic temperature fluctuations. Water intake can increase to as much as 2 gallons a day. The human body can only absorb 1 liter of water per hour in high temperatures and humidity. Most people are in a chronic state of dehydration and often mistake thirst for water as a craving for food, alcohol and caffeine.

DISINFECTING & PURIFYING

Always disinfect water when you can. Boiling is the most effective way to purify water. Boiling water will kill ALL biological contaminants, but will not remove chemicals, toxins, heavy metals or radioactivity. If you boil saltwater, the steam created is fresh water and if you boil all the water out, you are left with salt. Salt is important in all climates to maintain adequate electrolyte levels. To help replace electrolytes, add a small pinch of salt back into a liter of distilled water.

Iodine tincture 2% kills all biological contaminants except Cryptosporidium which comes from deer, goats, cows, sheep and elk. Pregnant women, children and those allergic to seafood should avoid this water purification method. Add 8-10 drops of iodine per liter of water and wait about 20 minutes.

Average household bleach containing 5% – 6% sodium hypochlorite disinfects water. Add bleach according to the chart below and wait 20 – 30 minutes before drinking. Bleach has a shelf life of no more than 1 year after its expiration date so rotating your stock is important. In an event that creates long term supply demands, it will most likely be an item that is initially available but over time become in high demand.

High Turbidity

Volume of Water to be Treated	Bleach Solution to Add
1 quart/1 liter	5 drops
1/2 gallon/2 quarts/2 liters	10 drops
1 gallon	1/4 teaspoon
5 gallons	1 teaspoon
10 gallons	2 teaspoons

Fig. 5-1 Bleach to Water Treatment

The chart above is for water that has high turbidity, such as muddy pond water or puddles. If the water you are disinfecting is clear to begin with, these amounts can be reduced in half.

Potassium permanganate (a.k.a. Condy's Crystals or KMNO4) disinfects bacteria from water. Add 3 – 4 crystals per liter of water and let sit for 2 hours. You want the water to be light pink which indicates enough potassium permanganate has been added to disinfect.

There are hundreds of water purification methods readily available on the market, whether tablet form, purification pumps or purification straws. Using iodine, bleach or potassium permanganate are recommended because they serve multiple purposes and are compact, easy to store methods. Knowing what surplus water supply you will be using can narrow your method. Be advised that due to the use of pesticides, mismanagement of industrial waste, boating accidents and other environmental hazards, many large bodies of water in the United States and abroad, such as Lake Michigan, the Mississippi River and the Potomac River are riddled with non-biological toxins that are not easily removed without specialized filtering systems. In some cases it is impossible to remove heavy metals/toxins to a safe drinking level, however if it is the only water available and you are on the verge of death from dehydration, you may want to drink it and deal with the toxicity concerns after you are rescued or out of the emergency situation.

Charcoal can be used to filter unwanted flavor and smell from water. Add charcoal to water when you boil it or pour water through a charcoal filter. This can be made by putting charcoal in a sock or piece of cloth and pouring the water through it and into a container.

Making a larger water filtration system is easy. This method does not purify all contaminants from water, but it will reduce biological and chemical toxins and remove odors. Gather three or four 5-gallon buckets. Punch small holes in the bottom of 3 of the buckets. Now you will want to almost half fill each bucket. The top one gets gravel. The next gets sand. The bottom of the last bucket gets a piece of fabric or non-toxic plant fibers and then crushed charcoal from a fire. Add a fine layer of sand at the bottom of this bucket too if feasible. Stack the buckets one on top of the other, top - gravel, middle - sand and bottom - charcoal. Pour water into the top bucket and let it filter through. It won't come out clear at first, so run the water through it repeatedly. It will eventually run clear. Again, this will not kill or remove all pathogens.

If you need to boil water and you do not have a fireproof container, fill a container, such as a 5-gallon bucket, about halfway with water. Line the container bottom with small rocks (do not use sticks unless you are certain they are non-toxic and not poisonous) to protect the container from melting, and then add hot rocks from your fire into the container until the water bubbles and boils. Filter through a cloth or the above-mentioned filtration system to remove debris.

SOLAR STILLS & TRANSPIRATION

Transpiration devices can be made by using a plastic bag (no need to be clear) and filling them with non-toxic non-poisonous vegetation, Fill the bag with leaves, grass or other plant material such as roots, blow up the bag to add lots of air, tie of the bag and leave in the sun. This won't work so well in cold climates. In warm climates, the heat from the bag being sealed will cause the plant material to evaporate moisture. If your plant material was nontoxic/non-poisonous you will reclaim a small amount of water that has been evaporated from the plant material in the bag. This process will not yield much water, but a little something is better than nothing.

A distillation device can be made for both salt and fresh water, By using a clear plastic water bottle, you can create a solar distillation device. In an even circle, cut the bottom 3rd off of the clear plastic water bottle. Take top 2/3rds portion of the bottle and make a 2 inch fold to the inside of the bottle. Fill up the 1/3 cutoff bottom with saltwater. Place the 2/3 top of the bottle over the bottom 1/3. Bury your bottle distiller in direct sun about 1 inch into the sand. The saltwater will evaporate and collect on the top 2/3rds portion of the bottle and potable water will run down the inside the top portion of the bottle into the portion you folded inside and up. To get the clean, distilled water out, unscrew the top and pour out into another vessel. This will provide you with a few teaspoons of water. For this method to be successful create multiple distillation devices. Fortunately (and unfortunately) you should have no problems finding plastic water bottles scattered on the beach.

CATCHMENT & STORAGE TRICKS

To create a large-scale catchment system, set up rain catch systems at your home. This can be done several different ways. Keep in mind that rainwater, while drinkable from the sky, becomes non-potable when running off a roof through bird feces, asphalt shingles, etc. Place barrels or buckets at the base of your gutter downspouts. When using a barrel, you may have to shorten the downspout to flow into the barrel. You can also place a tarp on the ground with the edge and corners elevated creating a large rain catch vessel. Cover the water catch with a screen or porous fabric to reduce contaminates. Even an umbrella turned upside down in the rain can catch a couple gallons if diverted into a 5-gallon bucket.

A condom fits in your pocket or wallet and can hold over a liter of water. Non-lubricated and non-spermicidal are recommended if the water will be for drinking. To fill from a creek or standing water, stretch open and scoop quickly the first time, then with gentle strokes after to fill. Use a slip knot to secure and easily open. Add a tied-up T-shirt or a sock to make a great "water filled condom" holder.

If a power outage is possible due to inclement weather, fill up your tub, sinks, pots and buckets with water so you have plenty for drinking, cooking and flushing toilets.

The bladder inside of a box o' wine or box o' coffee makes a great short term or emergency water bladder. Simply pull out the nozzle, wash out the pouch and nozzle, fill with water and replace nozzle. They aren't tough, so protect it from pokes, abrasions and heat. Re-insert into the box or find a pillowcase. Attach tubing and make a homemade camelback. Use a plug or crimp the end of your tubing to keep water in the line.

TIP!

Carry a completely metal water bottle that is capable of boiling water in a fire. Do not use double wall or lined thermoses or bottles. The linings are usually made of plastic and will melt. Do not boil with a plastic top on. Wait for the container to cool (or cool it in a creek or in snow) before replacing a plastic top. Wide mouth bottles are more versatile than narrow ones.

TRAP!

Some people say that drinking your own urine can save you from dehydration. Don't rely on this. If you are already dehydrated, your urine may contain more salt, urea and uric acid than water and can be toxic to consume. If your dehydration has become severe it is probably okay to wet your mouth with urine. If urine is the ONLY liquid available to you, use distillation, a water purification pump or solar still to purify it and yield some lifesaving water.

A healthier alternative is to place a small stone or button in your mouth. This will create a small amount of saliva and give you some physical and psychological comfort. It is a trick the Australian Aboriginals have used for thousands of years.

HYDRATION TIPS!

Electrolytes are important to the body's digestive, nervous, cardiac and muscular systems. Electrolytes are sodium, chloride, potassium, magnesium and calcium and are all lost from the body through sweating. Even if you are taking in water, low levels of electrolytes impact your body's ability to properly use water. If you find yourself in an area where it is not easy to replace these, licking or scraping and consuming your own sweat (or someone else's) will mitigate some of your electrolyte loss and therefore keep you more hydrated and better functioning.

If you have made potable water from saltwater by distillation it is important to add a few drops of saltwater back in to replace some of the much-needed electrolytes. Another option is to take extremely small sips of saltwater.

Chapter 6
Tools

All tools are meant to make a job easier. Some tools you keep in your head, some in your bag and some by your side.

In an emergency items that did not have much value before, can be life savers. Learn to be creative and learn how to improvise. Improvising is a way of thinking; it is a tool.

The first tool in your survival kit is your will to live; the second is your ability to think outside the box. A positive attitude and hope are also crucial to your survival. You can have all the gear and food in the world but without the knowledge, will or desire to use them efficiently and effectively, you may not survive.

Having a spiritual practice in your life is a great coping tool. It boosts your emotional and psychological wellbeing in times of stress and fear. Feeling overwhelmed with fear can be debilitating and decrease your chances of survival. Regardless of your religion or beliefs, it is highly beneficial to release those fears and trust that you will be okay.

A trusted partner can often be your best survival tool. Working together in a survival scenario can mean the difference between life and death. Injuries, challenging terrain, emotional and psychological wellbeing are more easily overcome with helping hands.

There is no better teacher than experience, get outside and know how well your survival skills and gear work before you need them.

There are 3 simple machines that make up all mechanical workings. They are the lever and fulcrum, the inclined plane or wedge and the wheel, axle, or pulley. Whether you are splitting wood, using a shovel or using a bow drill, you are using simple machines to complete the task.

TIPS ABOUT TOOLS

When purchasing outdoor gear such as knives, bandanas, lighters, compasses, etc. select bright colors such as orange and red or add bright paint or tape to your tools, so when you lay them down or drop them, they will be easily found.

Two of the most dangerous tools in bush craft are the short axe (a.k.a. boys' axe, or small forest axe) and the machete. These durable, short tools can withstand the full energy your swing. When used standing fully erect, if you miss your target or strike a glancing blow, you can potentially hit yourself in the lower leg. Any mishap and severe self-injury could occur. Using them from a kneeling position can help minimize your risk, as the tool will contact the ground before your body.

Bone, antler and wood can be processed into tools using fire and stone or sand. For example, a wooden spear tip heated in the fire and ground against stone will create a fire-hardened, sharp tip. Coals from a fire can be placed on a larger piece of wood to burn out a concavity or a hole to create a bowl, container or even a canoe. Sand rubbed into the cavity of a bowl will refine to a smooth finish.

ONE TOOL OPTION

In the survival community, there is always talk about peoples' preferences for a one tool option. We couldn't publish this book without weighing in on this hotly debated topic. Our personal pick for the one tool option is the 12" Ontario machete straight back with a top swage edge. Ontario is an American cutlery company known for its legendary world class quality and budget-friendly prices. This machete has a blaze orange handle, that is good for visibility, with a D-shaped hand guard. . If by chance there comes a need to tone down the blaze orange, it can always be painted or taped over. The 12" along with a stone and diamond sharpener in the sheath goes with us everywhere. The size and weight make it less strenuous to use for long periods of time and much easier to manage when choking up on the blade for finer tasks such as carving or dressing game. Grind a portion of the back of the blade to a hard 90° for scraping and using with a ferrocium rod. The 12" is almost as effective for heavy chopping as a larger model, but far easier to stop when clearing trail. They are also very inexpensive and durable to the point of being bullet proof. Another feature is the hand guard that prevents slipping or flinging the blade away. Keep a Scandinavian edge on the tip and lower portion for slicing (a Scandinavian grind is a flat grind that makes the edge extremely thin and is intended for sharpening on a flat stone in an outdoor environment). Keep a convex edge on the middle-curved portion or belly for chopping. A convex edge has a bevel on each side of the blade is slightly rounded out from the cutting edge.

If you like to put your hands on the back of the blade or will baton the back of it, have a 90° angle on the back edges to create a flat surface. Having a saw blade on the back reduces the uses of the machete. If you feel strongly about having a saw, then get a machete and bow saw blade with a cover of equal or lesser length then slide it into the machete sheath. When you need to use the saw, you can make an on-site handle using a curved or angled stick. As a side note, making a usable handle for a 12" saw is actually more difficult than one for a longer length. Keeping a wire saw in your machete sheath is also an option. Since so many people have different methods and opinions, it is highly recommended to view videos on machete modifications as suited to your climate and geography.

KNIFE TIPS!

To settle the debate on the best survival knife...... it is simply, the one that you have with you.

A dull knife is a dangerous knife. Sharpening or profiling refers to the bevel or grind of the knife. Honing is what most people meaning when they say sharpening. A knife should be sharpened or profiled once and from there out, just honed. Always keep your knife honed by carrying a honing stone (aka sharpening or wet stone) with your knife.
A good bush knife is a tool that YOU personally understand, know how to use and is of reasonable and reliable quality. Pick a full tang knife

with steel running the full length of the handle, therefore the entire knife is made of one continuous piece of steel. It needs to be a straight blade of 4" to 6" and have adequate thickness to withstand your force when batoning or prying. A quality knife does not mean expensive. A truly good and worthy bush knife can be bought for between $15 to $75. Use your own judgment for what tool suits you and your needs. Mora brand knives are highly recommended for their extraordinary quality, reasonable price and variety of sizes, handles and sheaths and lifetime warranty.

A Swiss army knife or multi tool is the cat's meow in a survival scenario. Get one. Don't buy a cheap one. It is worth the investment to have a dependable, quality tool. Features to include among your other personal preferences are: a saw, a file, plyers and an awl.

Having multiple tools that will do all of the jobs and give you redundancy in your kit is better than a one tool option. Take care of your tools and they will take care of you.

Carry more than one knife. There are many different blade styles, designs and materials depending on the intended purpose. Have a junker knife for nasty hard jobs. It saves your sharp knife for when you really need it. A tanto/chisel tip with about half serration on the blade is versatile and serves well in day to day activities.

TRAP!

So many times, in movies, we see actors thrust their knives and swords into the ground. Never, ever put a knife in the ground or cut on a rock or metal. It will definitely dull if not permanently damage the sharp edge. If you need a temporary location for your knife, stick it into a tree or stump.

DON'T HAVE THE TOOL?
IMPLEMENT THESE TRICKS

Opening a Can

If you don't have a knife or can opener it does not mean you cannot get into that can. Turn it upside down and rub the top of the can on concrete, asphalt, or a rock for a few minutes, by doing this it will abrade the crimped top and allow it to open.

Make an Emergency Wire Saw

Not all wires are created equal, some experimentation may be necessary to figure out what works best. Take 2 small sticks 3" – 4" long and about an inch around, fold the wire creating a loop and place one stick into that loop, twist and connect the "open" end of the wire and place the second stick in it. These will be your handles. Take the wires and twist them together, using the handles to help you turn it. Try to maintain the twist as tight as possible, you want ridges. This is basically a reverse wrap cordage method using wire. Wrap the wire around the object you want to cut and pull back and forth. Be aware that using this will create a great deal of heat and the wire may get hot, lose its temper and break You may have to take breaks or give it a dunk in some water to allow the wire to cool throughout the job

Make a Fishing Spear

Make a fishing or game spear out of stick. Find a green stick the length you desire, 6' or a little longer is recommended. Bamboo works great for this. Split it cross ways about 6" down its length at the business end. Lash the stick below this spot to prevent further splitting. Now separate the splits into individual quarters (split it more frequently if you want more than 4 tines or points) by placing two narrow twigs into the cross pattern. Push the twigs down to cause the quarters to separate. These can also be lashed to keep them in place. Now sharpen the tines you have created. For increased functionality create a barb on each tip. Be sure not to remove too much material during the original sharpening, because the next step, fire hardening the points causes them to dull. Now give it a final sharpening and go fishing. When one point dulls or breaks, it is easy re-sharpen or split in down further and repeat the hardening process. Primitive peoples would create multiple barbs down each tine allowing them to make quick fixes in the field.

KNOTS

Learn how to tie a trucker's hitch, a prusik knot, a bowline knot and a half hitch. All these knots are load bearing and can easily be untied after extreme pressure has been applied to them. These knots haul much larger loads vertically than would be expected.

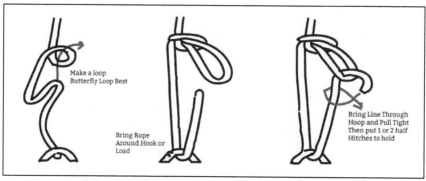

Fig. 6-1 Trucker's Hitch (public domain)

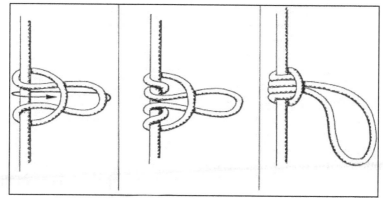

Fig. 6-2 Prusik Knot (public domain)

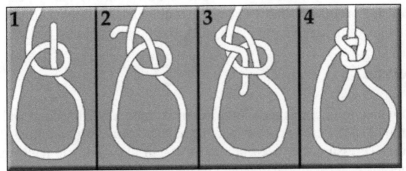

Fig. 6-3 Bowline Knot, (California Institute of Technology
Beckman Institute, Knots Glossary)

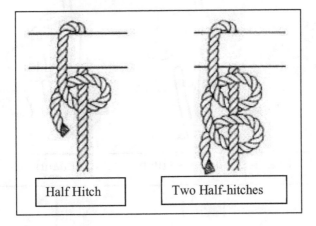

Half Hitch

Two Half-hitches

Fig. 6-4 Half Hitch (public domain)

WALKING STICK TIPS!

Make your walking stick taller than you are, especially if you are going
to put a point on it. You do not want stab yourself in the eye or throat
should you slip or fall. Always create the point on the edge of the stick,
not in the middle. The outer cambium is much harder than the middle,
making for a stronger point.

Using a section of PVC pipe you can create a walking stick and bow.
Store arrows and line along with other survival items inside the pipe.

Notch the ends of the pipe so you can secure your 550-chord bow string. Use end caps to keep the arrows in and protect the ends of the walking stick. You can find many videos online about this concept.

TUBE TIPS!

Tubing from exercise equipment, surgical equipment, elastic from undergarments or bungee cords can be made into projectile weapons; a very nice sling shot, a slightly modified adaptation of the bow, and combined with a flattened fork tip can make a Hawaiian sling spear.

Inner tubes can be a great resource because of their versatility. Add one to your BOB or EDC. Cutting it into rings creates rubber bands and ranger bands (heavy duty rubber bands). Cut in a spiral it creates a long piece of cordage. Cut off as much as you need leaving the rest in tube/container form. Take out the valve stem, replace with tubing and seal the joining opening and you have a camel back. It can be a tourniquet. It can be a waterproof container that can be resealed using heat. If you heat it to melting point you could patch a boat with it. It serves as a fire starter, accelerator and produces black smoke for signaling. It's a great asset in making traps and weapons when used as an action intensifier, such as a sling shot or Hawaiian sling.

MULTIPURPOSE TIPS!

Two space blankets and 13–15 ft. of duct tape can create a fantastically warm sleeping bag. The blankets can also serve as a rain catch or signaling device. Space blankets work by trapping your body heat and reflecting it back at you. However, it does not allow for water vapor from breathing and sweating to escape. To keep condensation away from you, stay clothed and/or line the bag with a wool blanket. They also make a crinkly noise that may or may not be of use to you.

Cigarettes, whether you smoke or not, can be a useful item in survival scenarios, a fire can be lit from the ember, mixed with saliva the tobacco is balm for insect bites and cuts and they are useful as trade and ice breakers during stressful situations. A potential foe may turn friend when you offer them a smoke.

For a slingshot, condoms (double up!), elastic from a bra or underwear, or a bungee cord and a Y shaped stick is all you need. If you are going to use elastic from undergarments or bungees, strip away the non-elastic material and then braid the elastic together to reinforce its strength.

Condoms can be a good place to store and keep tinder dry, especially in a wet climate.

Tampons and feminine pads can be used as fire tinder and wound dressing. The plastic sheath and wrapper can be turned into fishing bobbers or fire extender. The cotton and sheath can also be used as a straw to filter out water turbidity.

Sunglasses are valuable. Keep a pair with you to protect your eyes and keep visibility as high as possible. Protect your eyes from sun, wind, snow blindness, water reflection and debris.
Keep a hat with you. It is shade, a rain catch, and a thermo regulator. It can also provide concealment for clandestine activities.

A pair of pants can be turned into a backpack or floatation devise by tying the legs together and cinching the waist. Check out a couple videos for the most efficient ways to create these on-the-spot tools.

The umbrella is underrated. It is a walking stick, a shelter, a self-defense weapon, a rain catch, and shade from the hot sun. It is lightweight and small and can truly be a life saver. Keep one or 2 handy.

A scarf or wrap takes up little space and has multiple uses. Used as a head-cover to stay warm or out of the sun, as a face cover to filter dust, debris or smoke, as a bandage and as cordage. Its functionality is endless.

Carry a towel. It can be wrapped around you for warmth, it's a cover, it can keep you off the ground, it can protect your head, it can be used in self-defense (wet it to use as a club, whip or entanglement device, snap someone in the eye with it or put an object in the end of it, such as a stone, and it becomes a black jack or flail) Allow it to absorb water that you can wring out into a container. Dragging a part of it through the morning dew may yield enough water to be worth the effort. It can also be a signaling device and you when push really comes to shove you can dry off with it. Hitchhikers across the galaxy highly recommend carrying a towel.

Chapter 7
Firearms & Improvised Weapons
William Priday - Editorial

There are four rules that anyone who picks up, uses, owns or is thinking about procuring a firearm needs to understand.

1. <u>Always</u> treat <u>all</u> firearms as if they are loaded, whether you know it is or not.
2. Never allow the barrel of your firearm to be pointed at anything you are not willing to shoot.
3. Always consider what is between you and your target and what is behind your target.
4. Never put your finger on the trigger until you are ready to discharge the firearm.

Choosing a firearm is a very personal decision. It depends on many factors such as your intention, your experience/skill level and your geography. Consider these things when selecting the appropriate firearm for yourself. This is by no means meant to be a shooter's bible. These are basic guidelines and theories. I am sure that someone can come along and argue any given point. I am not claiming to be a firearms expert, I am just passing along my personal observations and opinions. Modern ammunition has become extremely diversified allowing all caliber of guns to have more potential.

PISTOLS

Pistols are for personal defense and come in a multitude of styles and ammunition capacities. Not all handguns are for personal defense but most of them are geared that way. Each distinct type of pistol has different pros and cons.

Breach loading, derringer style handguns are easily concealed and are essentially used in close quarters. Consider that a small handgun will be almost useless in a without rule of law (WROL) scenario, except as a one or two shot final backup or a sneak gun. They come in a wide variety of calibers and offer a compact concealment option for larger caliber choices. A wallet that has a finger hole cut out for derringer type handguns is available for ultimate concealment.

The pros to revolver style pistols are numerous; you can load it, leave it in your nightstand, pull it out a year later and expect it to fire. Its simple design makes it easy for anyone to use. Revolvers have robust construction, are easy to clean and when empty can be a bludgeon/club. The revolver cylinder construction allows for a potentially more powerful round than a semi-automatic. It also circumvents magazine or ammunition failures because the cylinder rotates and brings a new round into the firing position whether the previous round fired or not. On the downside, they are generally heavy. They almost always have lower ammunition carry capacity and even with a speed loader take considerably more time than a magazine feed to load. The recoil is more substantial than in an equally matched semi-automatic, resulting in taking more time to re-acquire your target between shots.

Semi-automatic pistols generally have less recoil, higher ammunition capacity and a higher rate of fire. The downside to a semi-automatic is the many moving parts which may more often cause jamming and misfires. Another con is a possible "failure to feed" problem. This can be caused by leaving your magazines fully loaded for long periods of time and not allowing them to rest. Failure to feed or ammunition issues can arise from firearm/magazine quality issue or simply a dirty weapon. Some semi-automatics and magazines simply do not like to fire certain brands of ammo. Taking this into consideration for a home and self-defense weapon, a firearm that may misfire or one that you need to leave the clips out of to ensure proper spring action is not a reliable weapon in the first place. Semi-auto pistols are generally more difficult to clean and more costly than other types of handguns. This not to say that semi-autos are inferior to revolvers they just have more variables. There are many semi-autos that have stellar performance and reliability with proven track records.

RIFLES AND SHOTGUNS

Rifles are your best bet for power, accuracy and range. Depending on the caliber, they can be difficult to carry with large quantities of ammunition. They can be bulkier and more challenging to conceal than other smaller choices. There are reliable take down models available that are optimal for your bug out bag.

Shotguns cover most of your basic self-defense needs, procure game and are a standard go-to. In short, they are hard to beat. On the downside they are heavy to carry and are limited in their range and ammunition capacity. The multitude of ammunition types make the shotgun the most versatile weapon, allowing you to take down anything you want. Manufacturers and citizens make everything from a slug to target/bird shot. Shotguns also come in a number of styles, from breach (single shot or double barrel) to manual operation, (pump or lever action) to semi-automatic, to fully-automatic where all you need to do is pull the trigger. They come in both smooth and rifled bores. Smooth bores are designed for "shot" (multiple pellets) and rifled bores for "slug" (a single bullet). They also come in a variety of gauges suitable for all different types of shooters. Gauges, barrel lengths, chokes and materials used to manufacture shotguns vary greatly in style and intent. As versatile as this weapon is, carrying it and a large quantity of ammunition for any great distance or length of time will make it your heaviest option. However, it is the gun most likely to do any job you need it to.

SHOTGUN SHELL TRICKS!

There are many ways to modify a plastic shot gun shell. One way is called a "cut shell." Cut just below the wad in a spiral motion all the way around the shell (Figure 6-1). A "cut shell" will discharge as one solid piece like a slug instead of scattering the shot. This is a great trick to know if you only have bird shot and need more fire power to take down larger game. (Disclaimer: There are no manufacturers that recommend altering firearm ammunition. This can be unsafe). Always check the barrel before and after shooting a cut shell for any debris, such as shell casings that can lead to misfire. Never load your shotgun with more than one cut shell at a time, because firing the first shot may actually cause separation in the barrel prior to firing. This can lead to barrel failure which means you just made a hand grenade.

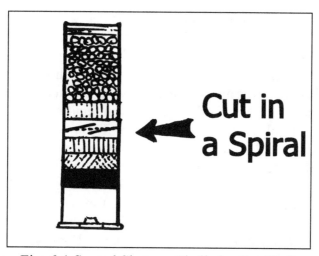

Fig. 6-1 Scored Shotgun Shell aka Cut Shell

Another interesting and useful method of altering shotgun shells is by waxing or gluing. This is done by cutting off the star pattern, aka business end, of your shot gun shell. Pour out most of the shot. Begin refilling the shell with wax/glue and your shot. The wax is a bonding agent. and the bird shot is like ballast. Place a small amount of wax in the bottom of the shell, next careful load with hot wax-shot or glue-shot mixture, tapping it as you load to settle the mixture. Fill to the top. Allow to cool and/or dry, then file the edge to remove excess wax and pellets. A dangling pellet could cause an unintentional primer strike in the tube. This round is best compared to a breaching round than any other type of ammunition, with one exception, it has the capacity to travel. When they hit, they fragment, displacing all of their energy into the target but the shot stays together until impact. Using this method will turn your "almost non-lethal" birdshot into a lethal round with greater range.

There are scores of videos on shotgun shell ammunition modification to amp up or customize your shot using anything from sand all the way to arrows. There are a few other classes of firearm that haven't been discussed: muzzle loaders, sub-machine guns or battle rifles. This is a topic that volumes are written on.

Consider guns by platforms. Choose rounds that works in a both rifle and a pistol. Granted, pistol rounds shot out of a rifle are not as effective as a true rifle round, but the ease of selecting one type of ammunition that fits both offers benefits you may not have thought of. Using standardized ammunition allows you to only have to stock and carry one type of ammunition. Standardizing your ammunition gives you the added benefit of only needing one re-loader if you decide you want to make you own ammo. And should you lose or lend out a weapon, your rounds are still useful in your other gun. Some pistols and rifles that use the same ammunition are .22 long rifle (LR) and magnum, 9mm, .357 magnum, .44 magnum, .45, both long colt (LC) and automatic colt pistol (ACP) and 410. There are other ammunition combinations that work, but the aforementioned are commonly available. Both .45LC and .410 ammo work individually in their respective guns, as they make pistols and rifles in .45LC and shotguns and pistols in .410. Specific firearm tolerances can affect these possibilities. A .45LC/.410 pistol (made in both derringer and revolver) will shoot a variety of .410 ammunition and .45LC pistol rounds. This may give you the best of both worlds. A .357 revolver will shoot .38 special rounds, but a .38 special will not shoot .357 rounds. The same can be said for .44 special and .44 magnum and .22short and .22LR in a revolver. They are all one way interchangeable. There are a number of rifles that will shoot pistol rounds, but most of them are lever or pump action, carbine or revolver style rifles. Of note, .45ACP and .45LC are not the same round. Don't ever shoot a shell rated higher than your gun will handle. Diversifications in modern ammunition types have led to drastic differences in performance. The age of your firearm is also a consideration, older firearms may not be rated to fire all modern types of ammunition. It cannot be stressed enough that diversity of modern ammunition varies so greatly that many smaller caliber firearms' performance can be pushed to a performance level of higher-powered firearms. For example, a .9mm with high performance ammunition can easily achieve the feet per second of a .357 magnum.

The .22 LR is highly recommended. At a combined weight of around 20 lbs. it is possible to carry a .22 rifle and .22 pistol and about 2,000 rounds that will fit both guns. While it may lack in punch, it is well known for its accuracy and in the hands of an experienced shooter it compensates for its lack of power with its speed and accuracy. Barrel length can also drastically alter the effect of ammunition. Specifically, .22 short barreled pistols do not provide the same results as a longer barreled pistol or rifle. If you are going to choose .22LR as your platform, give consideration to barrel length of the pistol and research the results of ammunition choice with barrel length. There are a number of high capacity models on the market and the rate of fire on some can be equivalent to that of a tactical weapon. Almost every large game species, from bear to moose in North America have been taken with a .22 LR. For as small as it is, the .22LR has a considerable fatality rate. They are extremely affordable, have low recoil and are easy to learn and use for people of all ages. However, the .22 does have a long-term downside, as they are rim fire and not a percussion cap or "center fire" the casings cannot be reloaded. It is however my favorite rifle when equipped with high capacity magazines. Using a .22 to kill medium to large game animals is illegal. It is considered to be inhumane, unless it is hit with a head or heart shot it can cause needless suffering.

Another option to consider would be a single or double barrel shot gun. This is more of a game procuring weapon. The 12-gauge shotgun is the most common ammo and the shells are reloadable with an assortment of items, from gravel to nails. Inserts can be purchased that fit down into the shotgun barrel which changes the chamber size to common .22 or .38 or 9mm depending on the insert kit. It gives the 12-gauge diversity and makes it a good complimentary weapon to the .22 rifle and .22 pistol.

Before you discharge, own, carry or handle a gun, check your local, state and federal hunting and gun use regulations. When considering buying a firearm, do your research, check with a variety of reliable sporting good and tactical stores, shooting ranges, firearms instructors and hunters.

All that being said, the right gun for you is one that you know how to use, are comfortable with and can operate with proficiency.

Disclaimer: I am not advocating or opposing the use of firearms in self-defense, nor the hunting of animals. I do, however, advocate your right to come to your own conclusion. This is simply advice. If you choose to have firearms as a part of your survival plan, don't look for other people's opinions or validation. In that sense, you should personally be educated, comfortable and confident with what you choose.

Different states and cities have different laws which may restrict or prohibit your ability to own or use a firearm. Check your local and state guidelines. It is <u>always your responsibility</u> to know the law.

TIP!

Carry more ammunition than you think you need when you go hunting, you may need it as a signaling device and you never know when you may be set upon by a pack of wolves.

GUN TRAPS!

Don't rely solely on firearms for protection. If you run out of ammo, a gun becomes a glorified club. Be sure to consider other weapons that you can easily find ammo for, such as slingshots, sling-bows, bows, crossbows, slings and bolos, etc. Also, when there is a need to stay quiet whether for hunting or to remain hidden, alternative weapons should be considered.

Silencers don't actually silence a gun like the movies. A silencer is a suppressor, like a muffler is for a car.

IMPROVISED WEAPONS

An alternative option for home defense, if firearms or other weapons are not on hand, is long-stream wasp or hornet spray. It is a loophole item. Places where mace or bear spray is illegal or not available or can be considered as carried with "intent to harm". Hornet or wasp spray is a household item, however, never declare that you keep the wasp spray on your nightstand with the intent to defend yourself. If you end up using it, you need to state that you were killing bugs earlier that day and it just happened to be there. There was no intention or premeditation to use it for self-defense. Keep a can handy and use it to repel an intruder, the solution is extremely toxic, can blind someone and will definitely stop a perpetrator in their tracks. Do not carry hornet or wasp spray in your vehicle or on your person, as that can be considered "intent to harm".

SLINGS

Slings, bolos and throwing clubs or sticks have been used to great effect throughout man's history. They are easier to construct than a bow and arrow, atlatl or javelin.

Slings have been used for thousands of years, are quickly and easily made, weigh almost nothing, takes up little room, have long distance range, is silent and the ammunition supply is endless. With practice, the sling can be a deadly weapon for hunting and self-defense. If you want to learn a primitive weapon skill, the sling is probably the most versatile and most worthy of the time invested to learn it. Constructing a sling is relatively easy, however it requires a lot of practice and skill to be effective.

SLINGSHOTS

Slingshots are a reliable alternative weapon that can quickly and easily be made on the move. Use a sturdy Y shaped stick and strong elastic bands, such as stretchy medical tubing, exercise bands or even the elastic bands from underwear or a sports bra. Add a reinforcement, such as denim or leather, to the very center of the band as your ammo pouch by creating a small slit on opposite sides of the material and then sliding it down the elastic band to the center. Attach the elastic band securely to each top of the Y by tying it on or create a narrow notch in the tops of the Y, sliding the elastic band down and reinforce with a knot on the front of the notch. If you're not up for making your own, store bought slingshots are extremely accurate and comfortable to use. As with other slings, the ammo is limitless. If you are not inclined to carry a gun, this may be a good alternative for you. With a little practice, you can become highly skilled and efficient.

BOLO

A bolo is a simple device made of 1- 3 strands of equal length rope with rocks or weights on the one of each end of the strand. Historically it has been used in open areas as an entanglement device and blunt force trauma weapon. Use it by holding the bolo in the middle or end, swing around your head and release towards the target.

PRACTICE!

Practice your chosen methods for self-defense, whether it be physical defense arts or weapons, both modern and primitive.

Believe it or not, there is a level of proficiency and skill needed to accurately throw a club or rock at a specific target. If you have children or a dog that fetches, get them to practice with you. Something as simple as a snowball fight or pitching practice can double as a method for practicing a survival skill. The more you practice, the better you get and the more confident you will be.

"If someone ever tries to kill you, you try and kill them right back"
– Mal, Firefly, "Our Mrs. Reynolds"

Chapter 8
Navigation, Travel & Signaling

When most humans get stressed out, lost, anxious, panicked or fearful for any reason, they tend to move very fast and erratically. In survival, unless there is eminent danger and impending doom, do not move fast. Haste brings complications and lends itself toward chaos. It is important to be quiet and to move slowly and remain calm. Moving too quick ultimately equates to a negative calorie gain. Moving slowly is the most efficient way to move. More opportunities for survival will come to you when you are staying aware.

When travelling into nature, even for a day hike, tell 2 trusted friends your plans and when to expect your return. Ninety-seven percent of rescues occur within the first 72 hours of searching. After that, most search and rescue missions become search and recovery missions. Leaving a note on the dashboard of your car has its pros and cons. By leaving a note with your destination and expected time of return, rescuers and officials can be prompted more quickly into a rescue scenario. On the downside, leaving this information publicly visible can leave you prey to predators or thieves. Use discretion based on your location and environment.

DAYTIME ORIENTATION TRICKS

An East-West orientation can be obtained by using a stick, pebbles and the sun (Fig. 8-1) Push a 2' stick into a flat patch of sunny ground at a 90° angle. Mark the tip of where the shadow falls with a pebble. Wait 15 minutes and place another pebble at the tip of where the shadow falls. Draw a line between the 2 pebbles. This line is oriented to the East and West. The longer you wait, the longer your space between markers will be and the more accurate your reading will be. You can also use a straight edge and hold it directly over the pebble markers to extend the line. The sun rises in the East and sets in the West. Once you know your East-West orientation, you can then determine North/South.

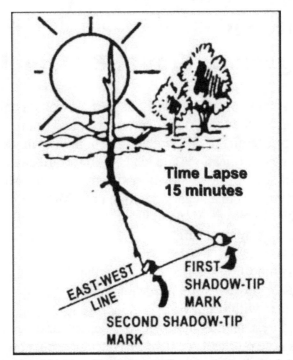

Fig. 8-1 East/West Direction (public domain)

A North-South orientation can be obtained by knowing what time it is. Point the hour hand of a watch or clock directly at the sun. If your watch or phone has a digital readout, draw a clock face with hour and minute hands set to the actual time. Halfway between where the hour hand is pointing and 12 on the watch face is the North-South Line. Once you have determined your North – South Line, consider the following image (Fig. 8-2) to determine which is North and which is South.

NIGHTIME ORIENTATION TRICKS!

The North Star does not move, all other stars rotate in a circle around it. Even if you cannot find the North Star you can still orient yourself at night. Find a thin forked stick, and a thin straight stick of similar length. Push the straight stick into the ground. Line it up with a star near the horizon. The forked stick is placed about 2'(feet) in the rear (as in a rear gun sight aperture) of the straight stick in the front. Line up the star, the

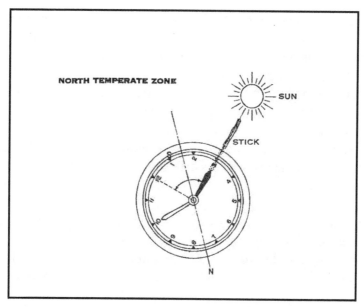

Fig. 8-2 Primitive Clock Face Direction Indicator (public domain)

top of the pointed stick and the Y of the forked stick. Try and imagine you have a rifle and are lining up your sights to shoot a star. You want to use a star near the horizon with greater movement, because stars closer to due North are circumpolar and will move in smaller circles. Watch to see which way the star moves from its original position for about 10 to 15 minutes. As the star moves, use the following directional key to decipher the direction you are facing.

Left	Up	Right	Down
North	East	South	West

If the star moved Right you would be facing South, if it moved Left and Up you would be oriented to the North East, Up and Right would be South East, etc. Remember the KEY to this is:

LURD
NESW

To ensure accuracy, repeat this process facing the opposite direction. Your findings should lead you to the same conclusion, if you have determined your orientation correctly both times. For example, if your original finding was that you were facing West, your second finding (now facing opposite) should show you are facing East. Stars closest to the poles are circumpolar and will give you a less clear reading. There is also the off chance you have oriented on Venus, Mars or another visible planet, which will not give an accurate reading. Make sure you repeat the process using several different stars in the sky to ensure an accurate reading.

Another way to find North is to start by identifying the Big Dipper in the sky and following the handle all the way to the far edge of the dipper and then straight to the North Star. The star at the lip is the brightest star in the big dipper constellation and sits opposite Cassiopeia as shown below.

Fig. 8-3 North Star Orientation (public domain)

The above image (Fig. 8-3) shows a view from North of the Equator where the sun is in the South, when South of the Equator the sun will be in the North.

Some of these tips lose effectiveness if you are close to the North or South pole. If you are lost near one of the poles, it's likely that direction is the least of your immediate worries. Compasses lose their effectiveness near the North pole, as they point to the magnetic North which is drifting towards Siberia at an unprecedented rate at the time of this publication.

If you see lights of civilization at night, mark the direction that you see them immediately, as the sun comes up you will most likely lose this bearing if it is not marked.

TIME

So, you don't wear a watch and your cell phone is dead, damaged or lost. To tell the time of day, or how much daylight you have left, hold your hand flat, palm facing you, with your fingers parallel to the horizon, stacking your hands one on top the other, between the horizon and setting sun, allowing 15 minutes for each finger, will give you the approximate hours of daylight left.

ROAD NAVIGATION TRICKS!

In the United States, you can tell whether an interstate highway runs north–south or east–west by its one or two-digit number. Although, in some cases an interstate doesn't run exactly north to south or east to west, the number was assigned based on the road's general direction.

Odd-numbered interstates run north–south, and the numbers increase as you travel from the West Coast (I-5) to the East coast (1-95).

Even-numbered interstates run east–west, and the numbers increase as you go from south (I-10) to north (1-94).

Interstate highways with three digits are those that connect to other major highways and interstates.

If the first number is an even number, it means the highway connects to another interstate highway at both ends, such as a beltway or a loop around a city.

If the first digit is an odd number, the highway is usually a spur route, which means it connects with an interstate at one end only, for example, a road that goes into a city.

LOST - SELF RESCUE

As soon as you realize you have become lost or even suspect it, STOP! Don't panic. Take a deep slow breath. Humans in a state of panic and fear make awful choices more often than not. You are going to want to do something immediately. And the thing to do is to S.T.O.P. = Stop! Think! Observe! Plan! If you just take off in a direction that you *think* you should go, you may get even MORE lost. If you made the mistake of not doing a time check when you started your hike, take a moment and estimate how long you have been on the move away from your vehicle, cabin or starting point. This is a huge psychological advantage. If you are 2 hours into your hike and realize you are not in the place you should be, you are only at this moment 2 hours away from safety. Before moving, create a highly visible landmark: 3 poles lashed together or a T-shirt on a tree branch or a distinct pile of rocks. (Surveyors tape is excellent for trail marking; it takes up little room in your pack and goes a long way.) The landmark you create gives you an orientation spot. By walking in expanding concentric circles (like a spiral or a bull's-eye) it can help you find your original incoming trail and keep you oriented to the point you first got lost. Keep your marker in sight. If you get to the spot where you are close to not being able to see your 1st marker, make another obvious marker and continue.

Always mark the paths you make or take if someone is injured and one person goes for help – this is of the utmost importance. We have heard of countless stories where the rescuers never find the injured person in the woods, even when the person who went for help had been there with them. They just cannot find their way back without markers.

Blazing is a good way to mark your trail in a survival situation. Cut a mark into the tree on the 2 opposing sides in the direction of travel. Or break a branch, but leave it attached so that its appearance is unnatural, so you can see it either coming or going. In this way, if your rescuers locate your trail, they can follow you and you can find your way back to where you originally started should your venture not pan out. Please don't go tromping through the woods breaking branches or blazing trees unless you are in an emergency.

One way to track and know the distance you have traveled is to make 10 marker strips with pieces of cloth, plastic grocery bags, surveyors' tape or whatever you have that is visible and loop them in your belt. Start walking and count every 50 steps. Then mark you trail by tying a marker at eye level. For every 10 markers you set, tie an additional marker to the other side of your belt to keep track of how far you have moved. That first marker on your belt signifies you have now travelled 500 paces from your original location. Stop, cut 10 more markers; this allows you to rest and to observe your current surroundings. You may see something you might not have if you were moving. Mark every 100 steps or fewer if this suits you or the terrain better.

If you are in dense terrain instead of counting your paces, it may be more appropriate to use the Hansel and Gretel method, which means whichever direction you go, as soon as your last marker is about out of sight, put up another marker. By marking your trail, you can always find your way back to where you first got lost so you don't get more lost and if someone picks up your trail, they can follow you.

SELF RESCUE - TRAP!

Almost everyone has one leg slightly longer than the other or that they favor. Believe it or not, people will sometimes walk in a large circle over the course of a day. If there is no visually distant point to bear toward and you want to travel in a given direction, use "line of site". As you travel place a marker just before your 2 previous markers are out of site. Always keep the 2 previous markers in site and in line with your current position, this will assure you are travelling in a straight line.

MEASURING HEIGHT TRICK

This method uses shadows and ratios to quickly find the height of a tree or a cliff that has a shadow. Find a stick that you are almost certain of its length. For example, you may know your foot is 10" long – you can estimate a 12" stick from this, remember to also account that you need a couple inches of the stick in the ground. Or you may know that your arm is exactly 2' long, find a stick the length of your arm plus a couple inches. After pushing the stick into the ground at a 90° angle. Measure the length of the <u>shadow</u> that the stick casts. Write this number down (in the dirt if necessary). Next, measure the length of the <u>shadow</u> of the tree or cliff you want to measure by pacing it out.

Now use the existing numbers to figure out the ratio of shadow to object height. For example, a 12" stick casts a 6" shadow, you estimated the shadow of the tree is approximately 30', you now know that the tree is approximately 60' tall.

$$\frac{12"}{6"} = \frac{X}{30'}$$

Keep in mind that it is not always going to fall as cleanly as a 2:1 ratio and when measuring a cliff face you probably won't have a rigid right angle at the base, which will skew the measurement. This is an estimate. Why is this important? Let's say you know which way you must go. Let's say a weaker individual is with you. You come up to a cliff face. You know you can climb it, but are fairly certain your partner cannot and secondly, aren't sure whether you could safely return down if needed. This allows you to ascertain that you have enough rope to safely get your partner up or yourself back down. Often, there are rockfaces and cliffs you can climb up but you cannot climb down. If you cannot maintain 3 points of contact on descent, then don't try it without a rope or gear. Eighty percent of all climbing accidents happen on descent.

SIGNALING FOR RESCUE

We have all heard heart-breaking stories of people that have been lost or stranded. One that stands out is the Uruguayan rugby team plane crash in the Andes in 1972. Search and rescue planes flew directly over the wreckage and the survivors, but they were never located because of one major reason, the survivors did not create a distress signal that could be spotted from a distance. Knowing how to create an effective distress signal could mean the difference between a successful, quick rescue or dying a slow, painful death from dehydration, starvation and exposure to the elements.

The international distress signal is the repetition of 3's; 3 fires, 3 flags, 3 X's, 3 shots from a gun, 3 blasts on a horn, whistle or flashlight will indicate that you are in distress. When working with a visual signal, place the configuration at equilateral distances in a triangle or a straight line, as these shapes do not occur regularly in nature and will catch the eyes of rescuers.

If you spend a lot of time outdoors or travelling, knowing or carrying a chart of the international distress signals is helpful. One has been included in the appendix. You may need the signals for your own assistance, or to recognize them and assist others.

Morse code for Save Our Souls, widely known as SOS is: 3 dots (S), 3 dashes (O), and 3 dots (S):

● ● ● ▬ ▬ ▬ ● ● ●

A Morse code chart of the alphabet and numbers can also be found in the appendix at the back of this book.

Contrast in color and large movements are the keys to being spotted by rescue personnel.

Learn to use a signal mirror. Most come with the instructions on the back. If you don't have a signal mirror, any mirror will do. Put two fingers out in front of you in a "peace" or "victory" sign. Use your fingers to sight in on the target you want to flash. Now with the reflective surface of the mirror facing away from you bring the mirror up between your eyes and your sighted target. Angle the mirror until you get the suns reflection on your sight. Keep in mind your target's location in reference to the sun, you may need to pivot the mirror in more of a side to side motion, as well as up and down.

Carry a whistle. Yelling for help is definitely an option, but you will probably loose your voice quickly. If you are alone, not a big deal, but if you are with others, you need your voice to communicate vital information with them to survive.

Our faithful survival chemical, potassium permanganate can be added to water to create a purple dye for a contrasting signal on the snow or light-colored ground.

Create what is called a buzz saw signal by tying cordage to your flashlight and swinging it in a circle to create contrast and movement at nighttime. This signal can be seen by ground or air rescuers. Make sure it is securely tied or you could end up slinging your light into the great beyond or your survival partner's head.

A tire, a shoe, rubber floor mat or any rubber material is flammable and when caught on a fire will create thick, black smoke and creates aerial contrast and movement. This method is most effective on a calm, windless day and less effective in high winds. Always remember to deflate a tire before burning. As a side note, if you don't burn all your floor mats signaling for help, they serve as a moisture barrier and keep your butt dry and off the ground.

Three fires arranged in a regularly spaced row is an international distress signal. During the day, you can also attract attention with smoke. Green wood and leaves produce smoke, as do manmade materials like tires, flip flops, sneakers or any plastic or rubber material. Start a fire using dry wood and add smoke producing material once it gets going.

Flares are an obvious signaling tool, ignite and wave it over your head or move in a circle to attract attention.

Flare guns are much more effective than a flare, firing it up into the air allows you to clear visual obstructions and attract attention over several miles. Don't point it at your face or another person. They can definitely cause injury.

Flags can be easily improvised, a national flag flown upside down is considered a distress symbol. In more recent years, this can also indicate an abandoned ship, national dissidence or a sign of war subsequently not all countries recognize the inverted flag as a distress symbol. However, a knot tied in any flag, a white flag or a flag with a square and a circle on it are all considered international distress symbols. (Seafaring vessels usually carry a pre-made orange SOS flag containing a square and circle.)

The above-mentioned visual signals can work, but sometimes you'll need to communicate a more significant message to an aircraft. We've all seen movies where the actors use huge "SOS" signs on a beach to signal aircraft. These are only effective when there is contrast between the "SOS" and the background. In addition to "SOS" the symbols in Fig. 7-4 will convey vital ground-to-air information to rescuers. Create them with clothing, rocks, plants, sticks or anything else that's clearly visible.

When communicating with your arms, simply hold them up in a "Y" if you need help or with one arm raised and the other lowered, forming an "N" if you don't need help. There are more sophisticated hand signals out there for military types, but these few should be all you really need.

You will know that an airplane has spotted you when it tips its wings back and forth. This is internationally known as the pilot saying, "I see you."

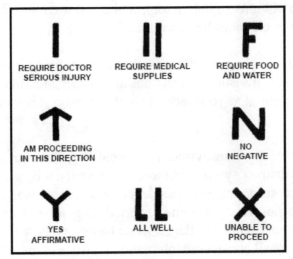

Fig. 8-4 Ground to air symbols (public domain)

STUDY UP

Volunteering to become an Emergency Medical Technician or Search and Rescue Team Member at your local Fire and Rescue department will get you free training in first aid, emergency response, and situational analysis. This gives you a chance to gain experience with emergency situations and help others in the process.

Chapter 9
Traps

Trapping has been used for thousands of years as a passive method of procuring food. No other way, except for fishing, can you have a lower output of energy with such a high return in calories. Knowing how traps work and where and how to set them is an invaluable resource for short and long-term sustainability. It is a skill you can depend on to feed yourself and your family. Understanding the animals and their habits will greatly increase your success rate. This chapter will discuss methods from a primitive angle, including the most useful, easy and productive trapping methods. Trap triggers and trap styles vary due to region, prey, predators and available materials. There are too many variations to cover in a chapter, however once you understand the basic types of traps and mechanisms, there really is no limit to how and what you trap.

TRAP TIPS!

Set up multiple traps, 10 – 20 will optimize your endeavors.

A packet of fishing leaders (steel, preferred because they can also be used for snaring) and strong cordage (550 cord, rope, bank line or Kevlar line/string) can easily be set up to take mammals, birds and fish with a fair amount of ease and a small amount of intelligence. Hooks will take turkeys, crows, seagulls, fish and small mammals with a good degree of efficiency in almost any environment.

Maintain your traps. The key to trapping or fishing is baiting for your prey consistently. Used conservatively a jar of peanut butter will bait multiple traps for months and most every animal likes it.

A fresh fallen snow is ideal for tracking and finding good locations for trap setting.

Light rain is also a great time to hunt or sneak around. The sound you make moving through the woods is muffled and the ground cover is softened, reducing crunching and crackling.

If you are looking for game and find signs of animals, move in concentric circles from that point to locate other signs and track the animal.

KEY TERMS

Engine: The object you are using to obtain force. Saplings, rocks, bungees and logs can all be engines.

Trigger: What holds the engine in place and will activate the tension and trap. It is the most important part of a trap to know and understand.

Activator: The object that sets off the trap or releases the trigger there by releasing the engines energy. This could be bait, a trip wire, platform, hole or noose set to entangle a target passing through it.

No Knife Traps

A no knife trap is a trap that can be created using sticks, string and/or wire without the use of a knife. Deadfall style traps use a weight to crush your prey by sheer force and are best for smaller animals. Different types of triggers can be used with the deadfall. Its ease and efficiency in set up and make it a favorite. Deadfalls are most often a baited trap. Animals like squirrels, chipmunks, rats, mice, raccoons, badgers, skunks, armadillos, wolverines, coypus (nutria), opossum, small alligators, birds, weasels, ground hogs, and birds could be potential targets. Use at least 3-4x the body weight of the animal you are trying to trap. You can get away with less but why go through the trouble for a half measure. Be wary of using too much weight because rupturing the gut sack can cause spoilage of the meat which in a survival situation is exactly what you don't want. These traps are limited only by the amount of weight you can lift and safely set a trigger to. Don't attempt to set up anything you can't lift with one hand. Use common sense and stay safe.

One thing you can do to increase the effectiveness of this style of trap (and decrease the required weight) is to use a hammer and anvil set up, a hard-bottom platform such as a large flat rock or board-like piece of wood at ground level as an anvil. The crushing weight comes down as a hammer and catches your prey between them.

Scissor Trigger Deadfall

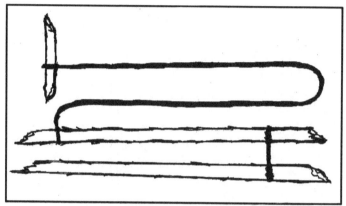

Fig. 9-1 Scissor Trigger Deadfall

What you need: 2 long sticks of equal length between 8" – 12" long and one short stick 3" – 4", which will be the bait stick. Tie the 2 long sticks together with a short piece of cordage (string, rope, handmade cordage, etc.) leaving about 1" between them. Then tie the short stick to the bottom of one of the long sticks with approximately 14" – 18" length of cordage. Find a large rock that is relatively flat on one side, one with a divot on one end is helpful for securing the trigger. Place 1 long stick vertical against or in the ground as your upright and wrap the long piece of string around the upright and then set your other long stick in place, keeping tension on the string as you set the bait stick as shown in the illustration below. This can be tricky to get in place all at once.

The scissor trigger is one of my favorite triggers. Primarily used for smaller game interested in bait. Lots of pros, but few cons. They are adjustable. The triggers can be made in bulk quickly around a fire at night. Just wrap up and bundle for easy packaging and separation while traveling. It is one of the easiest to set up on rocky ground as it doesn't have to be stuck into the ground to work, although it's easier if you can. The cons are that it takes 2 pieces of string to construct and slightly more knot tying and when setting the bait stick you really need to be careful not to crush your hand. At the final stage of setting this trap your hand

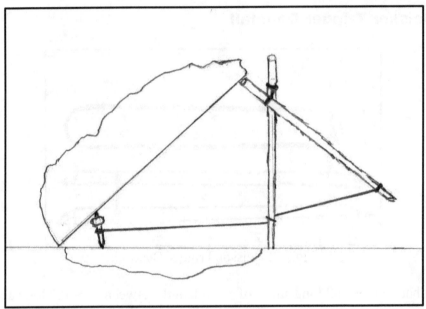

Fig. 9-2 Scissor Trigger Deadfall Set

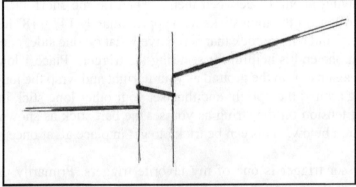

Fig. 9-3 Scissor Trigger Deadfall – Detail Upright Wrap

WILL be under the weight. Setting a deadfall in soft, sandy or muddy ground will decrease its effectiveness.

Taking up the slack and adjusting cord length is a bit frustrating for a novice. Often there is an almost endless session of cutting retying and measuring. You should make every attempt to never cut your cordage. Try and keep your line in one piece from the engine to the noose.

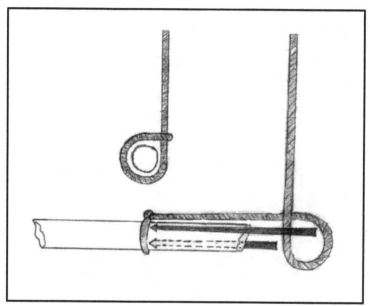

Fig. 9-4 Reduce string length without cutting

An easy fix for this issue is to loop the string back over itself, as shown above (Fig. 9-4) and onto the toggle or point of attachment. Do this as many times as necessary to effectively take up the slack or adjust the length.

Paiute Deadfall

The Paiute deadfall trigger is a favorite trigger for deadfalls. Anyone who can break sticks, tie a simple knot and skewer a hotdog on a stick can do it. It is by far the easiest and safest deadfall trap to set up. The upright support for this trap does not need to be stuck in the ground but it is much easier if it is and firmly so to keep it from tilting back. Make sure the upright support is clear of the rock's fall path; if it is set too close it can impede the rock from falling on the prey.

Figure 9-6 is an up-close illustration of the trigger, the toggle stick goes behind the upright, the cordage tie is on the side where the bait stick is set against the toggle stick and then wrapped around the front of the upright.

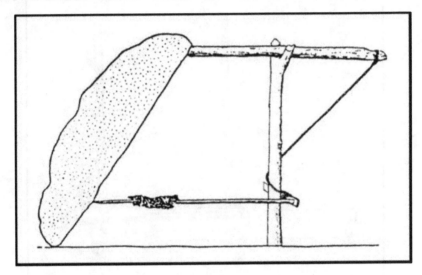

Fig. 9-5 Paiute Deadfall

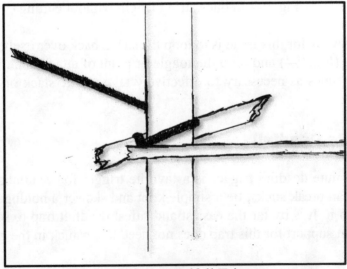

Fig. 9-6 Paiute Deadfall Trigger

Greasy String Deadfall

The greasy string deadfall is baited by rubbing or greasing the bait (mayo, worms, peanut butter, etc.) into the string itself. Once it has been chewed through; the supporting stick is no longer held in place and the rock falls, crushing your prey. It is very easy and safe to set up but once the trap is sprung the cordage used to hold the support in place will need to be replaced. This trap trigger method requires you to use more string each time it is set off, creating an equation of meat = cordage. Tie a piece of cordage around a stationary object and tie the other end to a forked stick. Place a rock with flat side down on the cordage and against the forked stick as shown in the illustration below.

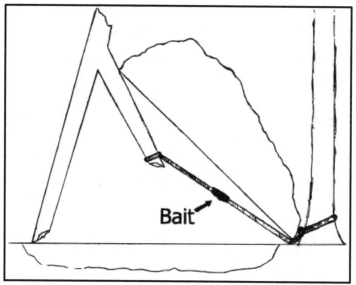

Fig. 9-7 Greasy String Deadfall Set

Snare

A snare is a noose hung in a choke point or path with the other end attached to a stationary object like a sapling tree log or peg pounded into the ground. Set this kind of trap on trails, paths, den sites or holes with recent scat or spoor or that your target is known to use. The idea is to hopefully catch your prey by the neck and strangle it, so set the noose at the same height as the animal's head. Use wire instead of string if you can. It is more effective because it tends to grab better and is less likely to be broken or chewed through and will maintain a fixed position during the set. String will need to be propped up by other forked sticks. Picture wire works great and can be picked up just about anywhere. It is flexible enough to be effective and tighten quickly yet rigid enough to hold its shape until the noose has been entered. Most animals instead of backing up when panicked will continue to push forward to escape. Make sure the other end of the noose is firmly anchored as the noose line will experience the full force of the animal in its attempts to escape. Rabbits, squirrels, game birds, muskrat, nutria and beaver are prime candidates for this type of trap. Deer and pigs can also be taken with a snare but require heavier tackle and a quicker response time on the trapper's part. This quick response is needed to humanely dispatch the animal before it suffers or escapes with injuries.

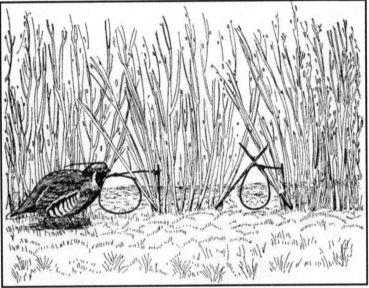

Fig. 9-8 Example of location for small game snare trap
(public domain)

Depending on what your set is for, when using wire for your noose, put an extra loop in the hitch. This allows the wire to collapse and lock in place. After copying the diagram in Figure 9-9 remove the stick by sliding it out and slide the other loose end of your wire through your double loop. This creates your noose loop, then attach your loose end to your anchor point, engine or trigger by twisting the wire enough around your connection point then itself. This is most useful when using flexible wire, if the wire is stiff, then it's not necessary.

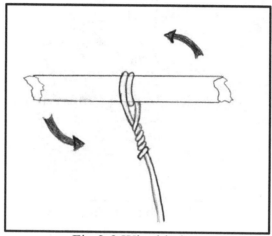

Fig 9-9 Wire hitch

Fig. 9-10 Funneling path for snare (public domain)

The path snare uses a branch semi-blocking the trail or run as a trip wire. Do not block the whole path with your stick. Use only enough to activate the trigger when the animal moves past it on the trail not totally discourage from passing through.

Fig. 9-11 Path Snare (public domain)

Twitch Up or Spring Snares

Spring snares typically use a sapling bent over as an engine to quickly snatch prey off the ground once they are set off. Rocks or logs can also be suspended as an engine to achieve the same result.

Figure 9-12 shows a spring snare trap set with a wire noose and sticks used as barriers to create a funnel. Whether baited or not deliberate funneling is needed to guide your prey into the set.

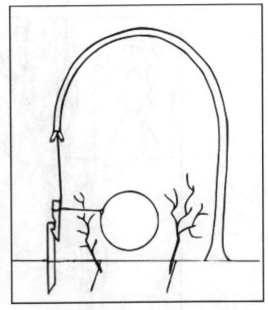

Fig. 9-12 Non-baited Spring Snare

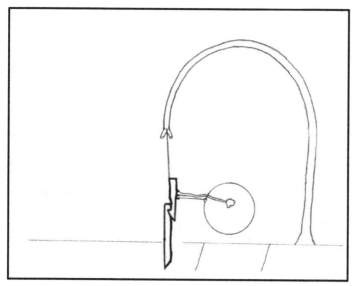

Fig. 9-13 Baited Spring Snare Wire Set

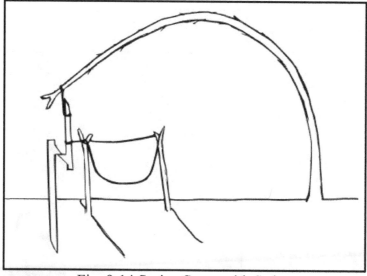

Fig. 9-14 Spring Snare with String

Figure 9-14 is a trail set spring snare (no bait) using string rather than wire, with sticks used to prop up the noose.

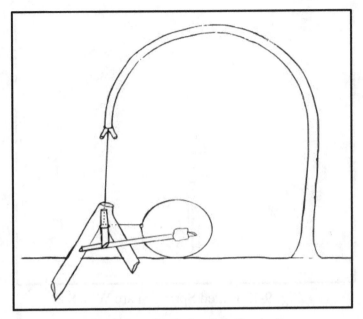

Fig. 9-15 Toggle Bait-stick Snare Set

Squirrel Pole

The squirrel pole is a variation on the ground snare. Attach multiple snares to a pole and lean the pole at a 45 angle against a tree that squirrels are feeding or nesting in. Squirrel nests will often look like large piles of leaves up in trees or holes in trunks. Squirrels, by nature are curious animals, take the path of least resistance and will investigate the new path

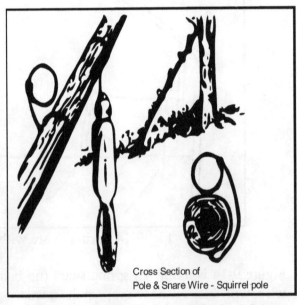

Cross Section of
Pole & Snare Wire - Squirrel pole

Fig. 9-16 Squirrel Pole (public domain)

you have created. Stagger the noose sets on top of your pole, making sure the anchor points of the snares are on the underside of the pole. In this way the squirrel falls off the pole and is strangled. For beaver, set multiple nooses at dam entrances under the water firmly anchored to a log or the dam itself. Use a "dive" stick or log on top of the water over your snares to force the beaver or muskrat under water and through the noose. Drowning is the idea here instead of suffocation, so keep the noose lines short to keep them from surfacing

Toggle Trigger - Platform Trap

The toggle trigger system is a personal favorite trigger. Its versatility can only be matched by the Figure 4 trigger which is described later in this chapter. When the animal runs up onto the platform to retrieve bait, it will cause the rock or log anchored above to drop and knock our or kill the animal.

The ease in creating and setting the toggle trigger and its multiple variations make it the "go to" for virtually everything. Deadfalls (such as the Paiute), platforms, spear, bow, fish and snare traps can all use this trigger system. This trigger system is only limited by the imagination.

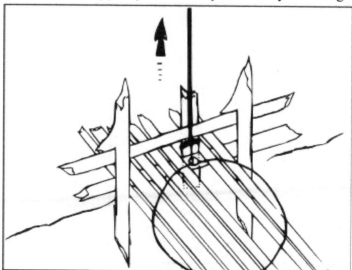

Fig. 9-17 Toggle Trigger Platform Trap Set

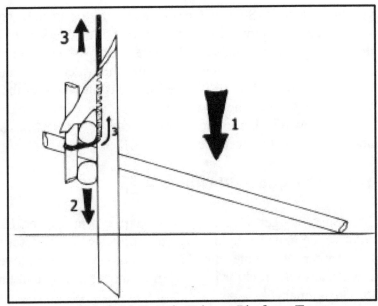

Fig. 9-18 Toggle Trigger Platform Trap

Fish & Crayfish Traps

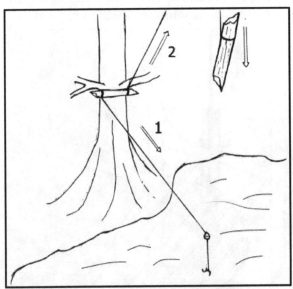

Fig. 9-20 Toggle Trigger Fish Trap

Figure 9-20 represents one of the easiest traps to set up. The key to this passive fish trap is having a hook. If you don't have a fish-hook, one can be made from a paperclip, a safety pin, or a piece of wire. If none of those items are at your disposal, a hook can be made by carving a small branch joint, a substantial thorn or a gorge hook.

Mouse traps can be very useful as triggers and taking a variety of small game. Figure 9-21 is a variation on the theme of thinking outside the box and could be used in a variety of ways.

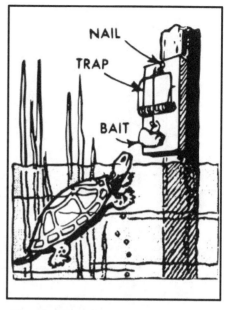

Fig. 9-21 Mouse Trap Versatility (public domain)

Dead Fall Cage / Live Trap – Arapuca Bird Trap

The Arapuca bird trap is a deadfall style live cage trap used for birds. This works best for birds because small animals can dig out from under it or if placed on solid ground or rock, they can chew through the sticks and destroy the trap. Almost any load bearing trigger that you would use for a deadfall can be used here. The only one that comes to mind that would not work is the greasy string trigger system, since birds wouldn't necessarily chew through string.

Start with two sticks of equal length. If you want a 3" cage start with sticks slightly longer. Tie the two sticks together at each end with cordage the same length as the sticks to make a square. Now turn 1 stick (the one on the right in the above image) end over end making what was the top now the bottom and creating an X with the string in the center as in the image below.

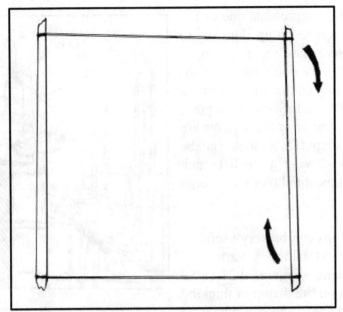

Fig. 9-22 Step 1 Dead Fall Cage

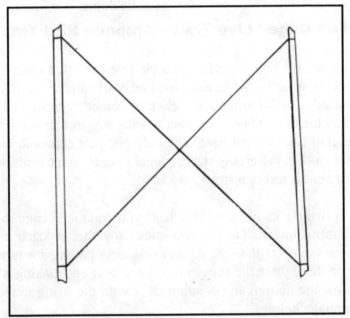

Fig. 9-23 Step 2 Dead Fall Cage

Once you have created your X begin inserting sticks one at a time, the
1st stick is placed on top of and perpendicular to the existing frame.
Under the string and over the stick. The 2nd stick will be placed at the
bottom of the frame, again under the string and over the frame sticks.
Continue adding sticks, weaving them between and perpendicular the
previous placed sticks and reducing them in size as you go to create a
basket type shape. As the sticks are stacked the string will lose slack
until the last shortest and uppermost stick finally removes all the slack
leaving you with a tight cage. Using this method of just stacking the
sticks under the string until taunt is not as strong as trying the ends of
all the sticks together. It does require much less cordage and if that's in
short supply should be the method you use. The cordage you use should
be heavy enough to hold the trap together once the trap is sprung. You
don't want it slamming to the ground and disintegrating on you and if
either string breaks using only pressure to hold the trap together it will
fail.

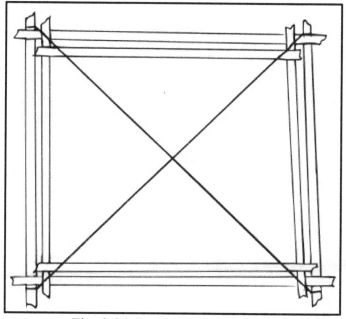

Fig. 9-24 Step 3 Dead Fall Cage

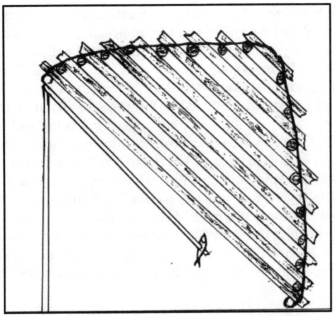

Fig. 9-25 Step 4 Dead Fall Cage

Continue until you have a basket shape as seen in profile in the image below. If setting this for a seagull or crow, fish can be used as bait. Any ground bird like turkey, grouse or quail etc. can be targets for this trap with the right bait. The trigger is self-explanatory using a bait stick placed precariously on top of an upright support and under the frame. The upright should not be stuck into the ground but simply resting on it. Since the frame is square, the back ends of the cage touching the ground will provide two points of contact and the bait stick on top of the upright provides the third, making it stable. Be sure to set this trap on level ground or flat surface to avoid an escape.

Knife Traps

Knife traps require using a knife to carve notches or holes in sticks and/or trees to create the trigger or trap itself.

Reverse Notch

A reverse notch can be made using a tree as the anchor instead You can see the removed notch on the left side of the tree for clarity not as a part of the set itself on the right. Use this method for larger game like deer or pigs where pounding a peg into the might not be possible or is not sufficient to hold the large amount of upward force applied by the engine.

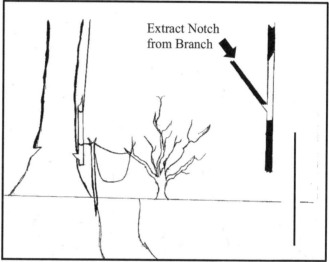

Extract Notch from Branch

Fig. 9-26 Reverse Knot Snare

Ojibwa Bird Trap

The Ojibwa bird snare is set near a place where birds are feeding in open areas without a multitude of places for them to land and observe their surroundings. Place the pole high enough for them to be able to land, rest, and observe their surroundings. Set up multiple poles close together. Often once one bird is trapped others will come to investigate and themselves be trapped. Occasionally the upright pole is also baited with whatever the birds are feeding on such as open pinecones, berries, or insects. Be sure not to use too much weight or you may just cut the feet off the bird and have it fly away and sadly doing neither of you any good.

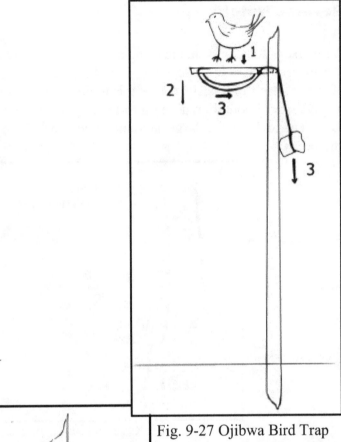

Fig. 9-27 Ojibwa Bird Trap

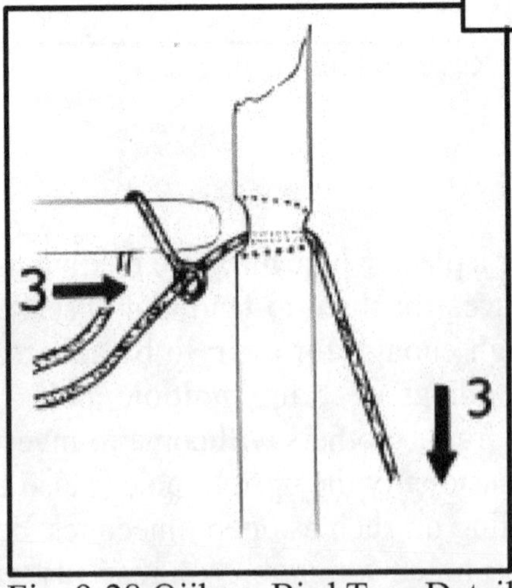

Fig. 9-28 Ojibwa Bird Trap Detail

Large Game Deadfall

To create a deadfall trap for deer or wild goats, a trip line is set across an animal trail and tied to a stick placed under 2 sticks that are tied together in an H shape and set around a tree. The deadfall mechanism is hanging over a branch and anchored to the H. The trip wire will create an up action against the animal's neck while the deadfall drops down on its head and/or neck.

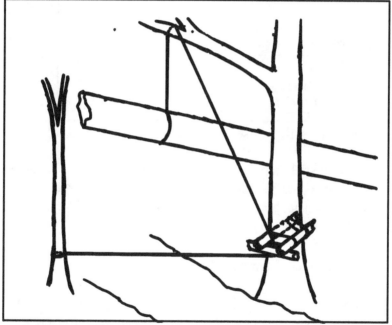

Fig. 9-29 Large Game Deadfall

Figure 4 Trigger

The figure 4 trigger is is one of the most versatile once it is mastered. However, it is precarious to set as the slightest touch will trip the trigger. The number of variations is of this trigger impressive. It is one of the only triggers that will support both upward and downward forces.

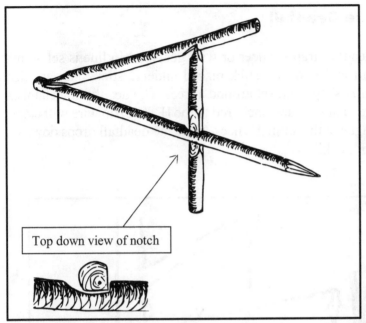

Top down view of notch

Fig. 9-30 Figure 4 trigger set for a load bearing or deadfall trap.

The horizontal stick is baited on the pointed end. Then a large heavy, flat rock balanced on the top stick. Make sure that the rock does not hang over the vertical upright stick as it will get caught and not fall directly on the critter you are looking to trap.

Choke Point or Funnel Trap

Choke points and funneling is the act of using natural or manmade obstacles to direct your prey into a pen or kill zone. Most creatures will use the path of least resistance. By placing an object of interest in the correct spot or narrowing the options a target can be coaxed or guided into the area you want them to be providing you with an opportunity to have them "spring" your trap.

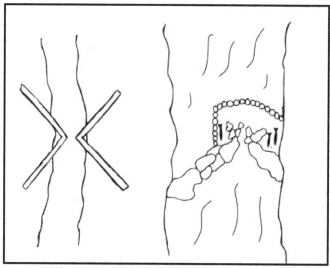

Fig. 9-31 Choke Point and Funneling

Fig. 9-32 is an example of taking advantage of a naturally occurring configuration for creating choke points for trapping fish. The larger rocks and log were obviously already there, and the smaller rocks and

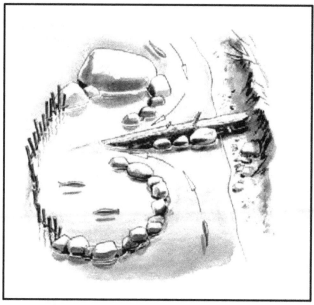

Fig. 9-32 Fish Trap (public domain)

109

sticks were added to create the desired shape. This simple trap made using rocks and sticks allows the fish in, but the design does not allow for them to determine their route of escape. This style can be used in both creeks and tidal areas. It is important to make sure there are no holes larger than your intended prey. Bait or scent can be used in this trap to lure the fish in. Once you have fish in the trap, block the exits and retrieve your catch. When you are done open the exits back up to re-use this set up over and over.

For tidal areas, just make a simple C shape with the opening towards the shore, build during low tide, allow high tide to come and go, then check for fish trapped inside

CLOSING

The most important skill to have is knowledge. It weighs nothing. Be prepared. Look at everything around you. Ask yourself not what it is, but what it can be. Being situationally aware, not paranoid, will start to train your mind in a way that makes you feel okay wherever you are, whatever you are facing. Keep your calm. Stay positive and be mindful of your thoughts and feelings. Breathe.

Don't forget your knife and your towel and may the force always be with you.

Aviation Body Signals
Ground to Aircraft

Fig, A-1

International Distress Signals

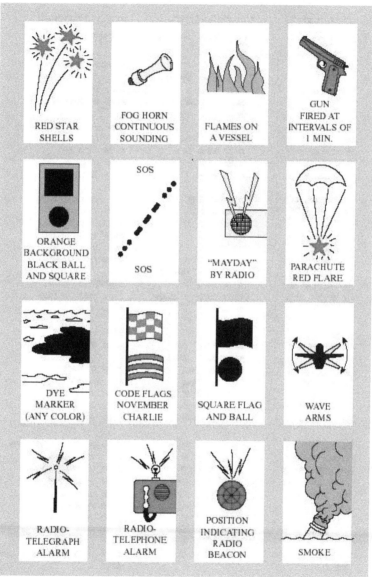

Fig. A-2

Morse Code

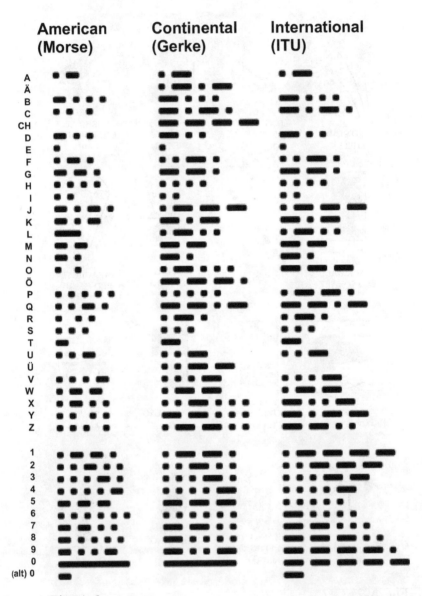

Fig. A-3

Maritime Warnings

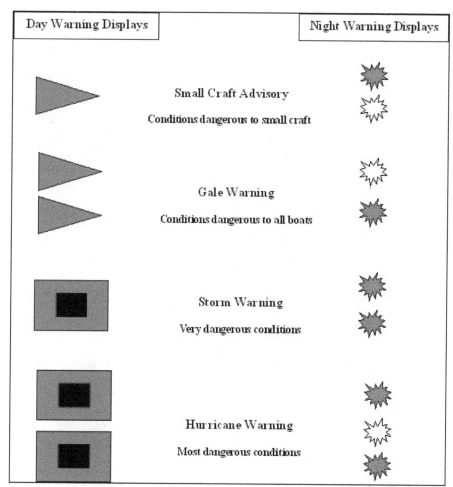

Fig. A-4

Periodic Table
of
Elements

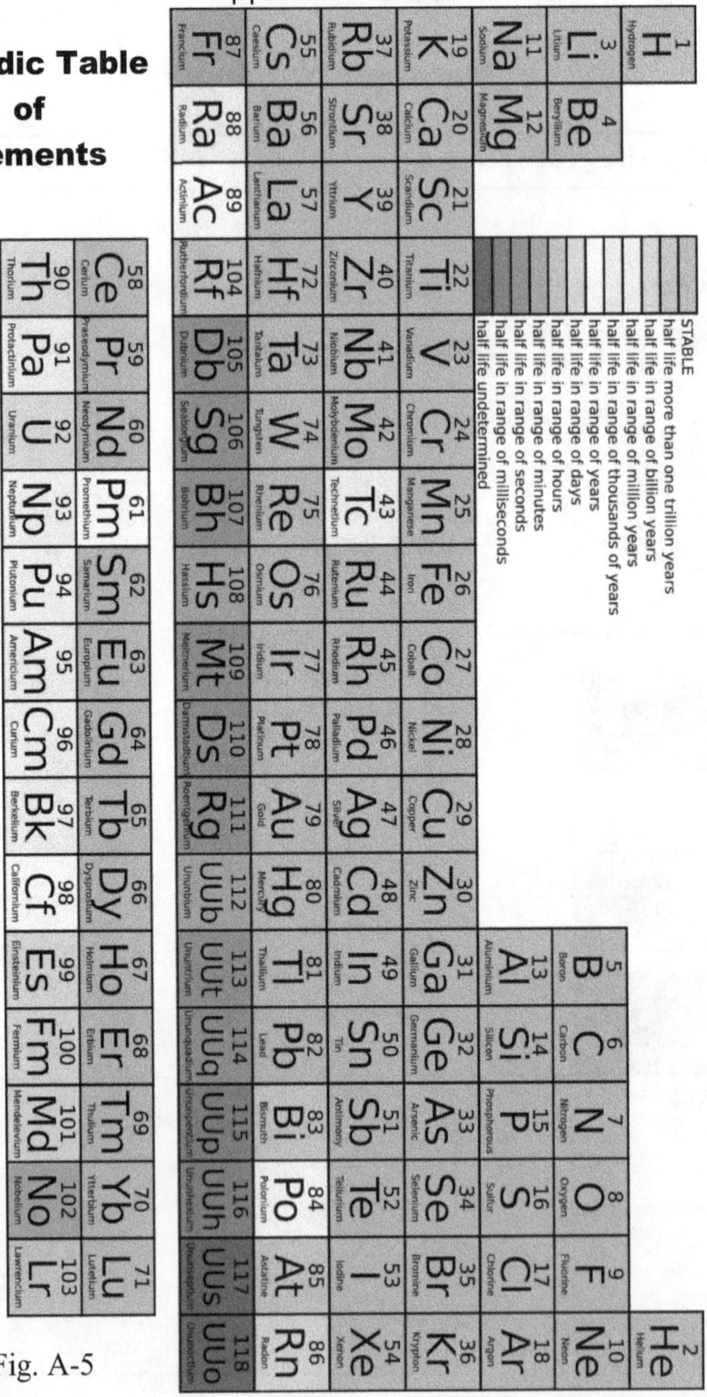

Legend:

- STABLE
- half life more than one trillion years
- half life in range of billion years
- half life in range of million years
- half life in range of thousands of years
- half life in range of years
- half life in range of days
- half life in range of hours
- half life in range of minutes
- half life in range of seconds
- half life in range of milliseconds
- half life undetermined

Fig. A-5

FIRE STARTER

FIRE STARTER

FIRE STARTER

FIRE STARTER

FIRE STARTER

FIRE STARTER

FIRE STARTER

FIRE STARTER

FIRE STARTER

FIRE STARTER

FIRE STARTER

FIRE STARTER

FIRE STARTER

FIRE STARTER

FIRE STARTER

FIRE STARTER

FIRE STARTER

FIRE STARTER

FIRE STARTER

FIRE STARTER

FIRE STARTER

Everytime
W^{II}

CPSIA information can be obtained
at www.ICGtesting.com
Printed in the USA
LVHW090108040520
654929LV00003B/757